# A Collector'
# Railwa

Edited by Handel Kardas

PUBLISHING

First published 2001

ISBN 0 7110 2617 3

© Ian Allan Publishing Ltd 2001

Published by Ian Allan Publishing

an imprint of Ian Allan Publishing Ltd, Hersham, Surrey KT12 4RG.
Printed by Ian Allan Printing Ltd, Hersham, Surrey KT12 4RG.

Code: 0106/B2

*An LNER silverplate menu holder, which would once
have graced the tables of restaurant cars as well as
lesser railway hotels.* **Tim Petchey**

# CONTENTS

**Picture Credits:**
Unless otherwise credited, the photographs in each chapter have been taken by the individual author of that chapter.

# INTRODUCTION

As these words are being penned, the railway press is full of reports that the record for a nameplate has been broken again, with prices now having broken through the £40,000 mark. Such figures could not have been conceived of 40 years ago when nameplates were regularly sold for a pittance and many were scrapped as a result of lack of interest. Hindsight is a wonderful attribute and there are no doubt countless enthusiasts reminiscing about their travels in the late 1950s and early 1960s and bemoaning the opportunities that were missed.

The past two decades have witnessed a phenomenal growth in interest in collecting of railwayana of all types — from the increasingly expensive nameplates to the more mundane items like paperwork and cutlery. Some of these items have an intrinsic value — there has always been an interest in clocks and the collecting of railway clocks, for example, is but an extension of this and silverware again has always been popular — but much of the railwayana available today has no value other than its relationship to the industry. Tickets, timetables and paperwork may have an interest to historians, but the only collectors eager to part with their hard-earned money will tend to be enthusiasts. It will be interesting to see whether, in the long term, prices will continue to increase or whether, as the current generation of collectors moves on, prices will fall. Just as those buying shares are warned that prices fall as well as increase inexorably, so there are countless tales from the antique business of interest in a particular area waning and prices falling.

This book, which was commissioned from Handel Kardas before his death, is designed to provide an overview of the most popular areas of collecting railwayana. Handel had selected acknowledged experts in the various fields to provide chapters. It can, however, be no more than a guide to a complex subject and, if you as a collector come across material in which you are interested but over which you have doubts, you should always consult an expert.

It is one of saddest facts about any field of popular collecting that there will be the unscrupulous, eager to make a fast buck out of the unwary. The production of replica or fake items means that it is often impossible to tell the real from the false. For the antique trade the key word is 'provenance'; unfortunately, for many elements of the railwayana market, provenance is the one thing that is lacking, since the tales of acquiring nameplates and other items via the back door are legion. As in any field of collecting, with railwayana it is always a case of *caveat emptor:* if a deal looks too good to be true then it probably is sensible to be wary. There are bargains to be had, no doubt, but there are also a number of those willing to exploit an individual's enthusiasm for a subject.

As readers of this book will be aware, Handel sadly died before he was able to complete work on the project and, probably, this is not the introduction he would have written. Without a doubt, however, he would have wished to thank his contributors for their work in the completion and we, as publishers, would wish to put on record our thanks to the individuals concerned for their help in seeing the book through to completion.

# CHAPTER 1

# LOCOMOTIVE NAMEPLATES

## by Ron White

Of all the features of the locomotive, the nameplate has always been, from our earliest train-spotting days, the first focal point. If we were too young to understand 90% of what we had seen or heard, if our parents/ grandparents were totally uninterested in what had passed before them (yet instinctively knowing that the infant would be attracted to/pacified by being parked not *too* close to a railway), a secondary instinct would coerce them into saying aloud whatever appeared on a brass plate. Thus it was that this writer could say, at a very early age, '*Lord Aberconway*', '*Robert H. Selbie*', '*Charles Jones*', and '*Brill*', without knowing what any of them meant. Only the village of Brill was known to my grandparents, and the status of the others was of no consequence whatsoever to them.

Life beside a short branch line did not allow for much variety, no other named locomotives ever percolated down the $3^3/_4$ miles of mainly 1 in 66 gradient, so my childhood horizons were not extended until I was old enough to go on the Sunday evening walk, an integral part of family life in the country before World War 2. By then, sombre LNER black had replaced the glowing Metropolitan Lake on my 'M2s' – I did not know at the time that they *were* 'M2s', or that their 0-6-4T wheel arrangement was a rare one in this country;

to me they were and always had been part of my daily life: familiar, almost boring. But the Sunday evening walk taken by my grandparents always led to a pub and preferably one by a station or on a bus route, so that we could get home. Suddenly, large green locomotives shared the double track of the Metropolitan and Great Central joint, as so many of the cast-iron notices declared it (themselves very collectable now had we but known, not that in those respectable times anyone would have dreamed of unbolting one). New, strange names to savour, *Lord Stuart of Wortley*, *Gerard Powys Dewhurst*, *Jutland* and *Ypres* on loudly bellowing machines with deep toned whistles, *Sansovino*, *Woolwinder*, *Tracery* and *Hermit* piping shrilly, and making the oddest of off-beat sounds, which I was unable to reconcile with the speed of the wheels going round.

There were very few books around in the late 1930s from which information could be gleaned. My eighth birthday was marked by a copy of *Locomotives of the LNER, Past & Present* (price 1s) and where that was found I do not know, but it is by me as I write, and what strange names *that* revealed from unknown railways marked simply as emanating from the 'North British Section'! Then came the war, and for a while I was reduced to overlooking our local goods yard full to the brim and the ever-dirtier

**Above:** *A display of GWR 'Saint' nameplates at the Great Western Society's Didcot Railway Centre. Brought together for a special occasion, this shows what a surprising number of plates have survived from relatively early withdrawals, indicating how long people have been collecting nameplates – luckily for the present.* **Author**

**Above:** *A fine display of 'Britannia' class plates (plus one 'Clan') at an exhibition. The range of grand-sounding names is right in the tradition going back to Ramsbottom & Webb on the LNWR, fittingly for a class so associated with LMS thinking.* **Author**

locomotives hauling ever-heavier trains.

On transferring to the local grammar school in 1942, I was enchanted to find that the Great Central ran sufficiently close to the buildings for the science lab windows to rattle in time with the thunderous exhaust of an overloaded 'B3' (the 10.00 and 15.20 Marylebone-Manchester could each run in three portions and each with 14 on) but the 'Sandringhams' would scarcely affect the windows at all; the 'V2s' were somewhere in between. All this was very interesting – rather more so than trying to absorb Boyle's Law – but the advent of the very first Ian Allan *ABCs* on the station bookstall was even more interesting. An academic career that was never really destined for high places went steadily down the tubes and my father annexed all my railway book collection, with the threat that he would burn it if I failed the School Certificate Matriculation – the sort of statement which concentrates the mind wonderfully! I duly got the necessary pieces of paper from Oxford.

So it was that I went into the City in 1948, to set up a career making a drama out of a crisis, on a salary of £104 per year. On that money I could not afford a season ticket but in those days Workmen's Tickets were available on trains starting before 07.30, and a Workman was anyone who could get up early enough. The fare for a round trip of 70 miles was 1s 5½d (7p) and a Weekly Workman's was 7s 6d (37½p) for six days (we worked two Saturday mornings out of three in those days but were permitted to wear sports jackets and flannels in lieu of the usual dark suit and starched collar).

On that sort of money it was not practical to start collecting nameplates, even though they were available from as little as 10 shillings (50p). Prices varied from Region to Region, with the more rapacious ones asking as much as £3 10s (£3.50). There were one or two shrewd persons of greater solvency who saw the possibility of nameplates becoming collector's items, and some very substantial investments (by the standards of the times) were made. But to be fair, they did keep a fair number for their own pleasure and the surplus, which came out onto an unsuspecting market, had been marked up but not unreasonably so. And since the majority of collectors were unaware that they could have bought direct (involving personal effort in fetching and carrying unwieldy lumps of metal by public transport), they were well content to let the nice, kind dealers do the preliminaries for them.

Collecting nameplates in those far-off days of the 1960s was a much simpler affair than it is today. Then, the dealers would issue substantial lists of plates at relatively affordable sums, and if a plate stuck around, it was frequently possible to negotiate a part-exchange, which is how I started my own modest collection. I had set myself modest criteria (I was already too late to play with the grown-ups) but it was quite a reasonable target to get a plate from each of the Big Four companies, plus a BR Standard (preferably a 'Britannia') and, if possible, a Great Central plate (and I was not too bothered about the class, though I would have preferred a Neasden locomotive). It was thought that this could be done for about £300 for all six, if one was not too particular about either names or classes. (Readers who buy at Sheffield Railwayana Auctions may, at this point, have hysterics or sob uncontrollably, as the mood takes them.)

My very first plate was a 'B1' – *Puku* – not the loveliest name but, at £42, a good lump of brass. The whole deal was for £50 and included a couple of GWR cabside numberplates and the odd worksplate, so all in all it was not too bad a start down the slippery slope. I was then informed that there was an 'unsellable' 'Jubilee' plate in the BR stores at Stoke and that George Dow, of blessed memory, was looking for a simple-minded person with £45 to rid him of this incubus. I duly did so, receiving, eventually, *Shovell* ex-No 45651. Stoke informed me that they had sent the plate by rail to Hemel Hempstead, who would deliver, but please could they have their tailor-made crate back? After some weeks I enquired why I had not received the plate; Stoke affirmed that it had been sent as promised, so heigh-ho to Hemel Hempstead to find it had been returned undeliverable, as our newish road did not appear on their street map! Eventually it turned up and I collected it, cracking open the case in the Guvnor's office and leaving him to clear up the splinters.

The next two, *Sir Prianius* and *Aston Hall,* nominally cost £65 each but in actual terms much less – I had a contract to restore *all* the plates in a major collection at £3 a time, and every time I had completed 22 I would get a modest plate for my services.

The 'Arthur' was no problem but finding the 'Hall' was; he had so many Western plates stacked against the walls like giant brass card indices and we went through them with the owner muttering, 'I know I've got one somewhere.' We tracked our way through a stack of 'Kings', 'Castles', *Viscount Churchill, The Great Bear*, a few 'Stars' and 'Saints', and eventually this poor little 'Hall' appeared and I bumbled off back down the Great North Road very happily. (I think there might have been one 'Grange' and one 'Manor' in there too but it really was a *very* comprehensive lot of the really good ones.)

The 'Britannia', *Ariel*, smallest of all the 'Britannia' plates, came from Mike Higson, then operating from Harrow-on-the-Hill, and was listed by him at £75. Mike had the delightful habit of having a Spring Sale, at which he knocked 20% off, thus bringing it down to £60 and into range. I also did restoration work for him and he owed me £2 10s, so I walked down the hill with this lovely little plate under my arm, on to the Met line and home, £57 10s worse off but very content, and I still have that one to this day.

The Great Central plate was probably the biggest bargain of them all. I had been looking after another collection while the owner was changing houses and eventually he offered me *Prince Albert* at £30. It was not a Neasden loco but it was a 'Director' and I had seen it, so I was able to over-rule myself without difficulty. All six plates of my target collection had scraped in just under budget by 1968.

Today, finding those six would probably cost £30,000, *if* they could be found. The advent of the specialised railwayana auction market has sent prices sky high and a new breed of collector has evolved. Plates *can* still be bought and sold privately but there are no bargains around these days, as even the national press has taken to reporting each new world record price for plates, as prices spiral ever upwards. As I write, the current record is £34,200 for *Duchess of Devonshire* (about

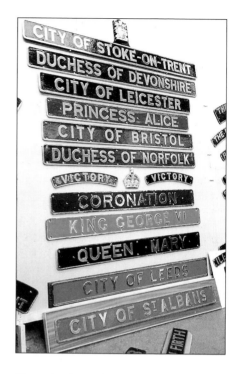

**Above:** *A quite mouth-watering display of plates from the 'Coronation' ('City' or 'Duchess') class Pacifics of the LMS. As most of this class survived into the early 1960s, a high proportion of the nameplates was saved.* **Author**

double what it cost to build the engine and tender in 1938!). If a private individual sells, he will almost certainly have a pretty shrewd idea of the going rate at Sheffield and the best one can hope to do is save the commission.

At least when buying at Sheffield one is usually sure that the plate is genuine and will be accompanied by the original paperwork where available. Other auction houses (Kidlington, Solent, Birmingham and Pershore are the familiar names) are pretty reliable too, but they tend not to get *la crème de la crème* and there is permanent demand for the very best. Ian Wright, proprietor of Sheffield Railwayana Auctions, knows where virtually every plate is and, should a replica turn up and be offered as an original, he will contact the owner of the original to check if his is the plate offered, if it has been stolen, or if it is a replica. The vast prices now commanded have brought about a considerable upsurge of replicas, which are *very* hard to detect – they are generally the merest fraction smaller than the original, due to shrinkage at casting. Replicas tend to be of the smaller plates, which are easier to cast and where shrinkage is less. *Caveat emptor!* I have urged the makers of such replicas to cast into the back some distinguishing mark but they decline, and they too say *caveat emptor*, which is not good enough to protect the innocent in an increasingly expensive hobby.

Anyone setting out on the path of nameplate collecting will need a little help and a lot of luck. Each Region has its own devotees, and when the really important plates come up for sale, there can be an undignified scramble and the sky's the limit.

*Above:* A plate from one of Hawksworth's under-appreciated 'County' class, this being from No 1023. Most unusually for the GWR, the plates were straight, as the class had continuous splashers. The size is apparent — this is a two-man lift! **Author**

## Western Region/GWR

These plates are very distinctive and handsome, with brass letters and beading riveted to an elegantly shaped steel

*Below:* 'Star' class No 4004 Morning Star nameplate. **Ian Allan Library**

backplate. The plates are heavy and need room to display. Older engines had full beading (wrapping round the backplate) but wartime and more recent classes *may* have half-beading (covering the face only). The half-beaders tend to be less popular. The lettering style is known as Egyptian face and has been used for ever. One tiny detail difference is that on earlier types the words 'of' or 'the' will be in a thin sans serif style, while on the later classes they will be in a reduced size of the standard Egyptian face.

An approximate pecking order of classes would be: 'King', 'Castle' (full-beading/half-beading), 'Star', 'County' (right-hand side with backplate, full-beading/half-beading) 'County' (left-hand side, no splasher, full-beading/half-beading), 'Saint', 'Lady', 'Court', 'Grange', 'Manor' (full-beading/half-beading).

The really old classes: 'Duke', 'Bulldog', 'Flower' tend to vary considerably and the 'Ringers' (combined name and number plate) are very sought after, especially those few with the GWR coat of arms in the centre.

I had intended to give a rough guideline on prices, but with matters escalating as they are any attempt would be doomed to failure. There is very little about at £8,000 these days.

**Above:** *Renamed 'Castle' class No 5017* The Gloucestershire Regiment 28th, 61st *nameplate and regimental badge.* **Ian Allan Library**

## London Midland Region/LMS

The straight 'Princess Coronation' plates hold the world record as I write. The first of these were chromium plated. Some restored examples have been rechromed and, of course, this covers the back as well. Unrestored examples will normally have lost all the chrome except for fragments under the bottom edge and on the ends. (These plates made excellent footholds for fitters trying to reach the dome or top-feed, and gritty hobnailed boots and chrome were incompatible.)

'Princess Royal' – a small class and plates rarely appear. These range from the domestic-size *Queen Maud* to the very heavy *Princess Arthur of Connaught* or *Princess Helena Victoria*. Either will require solid money on scarcity grounds.

'Royal Scot' plates are subdivided into several types. There are Badge Plates (*British Legion, Old Contemptibles*), double line with badge over, single line with badge over, double line with badge under, single line with badge under, double line no badge, single line no badge. Since the plates and badges were sold separately, complete sets are *very* desirable.

'Patriot' class plates fit the same categories and similar considerations apply.

**Above:** *Nameplate with Regimental badge on 'Royal Scot' No 46129. Again, the pairing is desirable. This was the only nameplate with badge above to have a distance piece raising it above the splasher.* **Brian Hilton/Author's Collection**

They are quite hard to find.

'Jubilees' are more common; only two with double lines, three single lines with badges (two of which are a little peculiar, *Southern Rhodesia* is the really good one), and 187 single lines of varying length and quality of name.

If you can find a complete set from any of the four named 'Black Fives', no one will believe you. Only one of the eight sets is known to have survived complete.

**Below:** *The nameplate and badge in place on 'Patriot' No 45507's driving splasher. The pairing is most desirable to a collector.* **Author**

## Eastern Region/LNER

Like the Midland, a mixture of straight and curved plates. Straight plates are always easier to display and handle; the great weight of the curved 'A3' and 'B17' plates demands a splasher on which to stand them, and should you be lucky enough to get a 'B17' Footballer set you will need the splasher for the half-football!

Pride of place must go to the 'A4' class, birds taking precedence over the director names. Do as I did: start with a director and part-exchange into a short bird plate, then a

long one. My sequence was: *Miles Beevor, Woodcock, Sparrow Hawk, Golden Eagle.* Remember that although many bird names were removed from the 'A4s', when they reappeared on 'A1s' they were *not* the same plates reused. The original 'A4' plates had genuine Gill Sans lettering, ½in wide. The 'A1s' had a debased style, with letters ⅝in wide, and they look less handsome. If the two *Kestrels* are compared (and *Kestrel* is the only 'A4' bird name known to survive), you will see what I mean.

The 'A2' variants had the clearer Gill Sans

12

**Above:** *Close-up of the nameplate for* Sir Nigel Gresley *on the side of the 'A4' Pacific.* **Ian Allan Library**

**Below:** *'V2' No 60847* St Peter's School York AD627 *nameplate mounted on the wall of the school.* **Ian Allan Library**

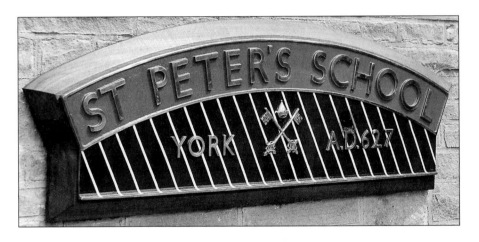

lettering and there are some very good names among them. The 'A1s' have an equally good variety but the lettering comment stands. Some of the longer names are extremely heavy and are not really domestic size – unless you are single and unattached, in which case, who is there to complain?

The 'A3s' are also brutes in the house. The castings are not of the best, the last batch bore Gill Sans lettering and looked all the better for it, but it is imperative to have a splasher made, since the ribs on the backs make them hard to stand against a wall and, should one fall forward, as they do, any

passing child or animal may not survive the impact. This applies also to the 'B17s' but not to the 'B2s' whose ribs were surgically removed when the locos were rebuilt.

The Great Central locomotives had a pleasantly old-fashioned style of serifed lettering. The smaller names had all the letters the same size; the longer ones had larger initial letters. Great Central plates formed part of the splasher beading and it is preferable to have part of that beading still attached. (This condition is quite often known as 'having ears'.) The 'B6' straight nameplates stood on top of the splashers and were bolted directly

**Above:** *One of the collectors' classics: a 'Footballer' name complete with half-football, on an LNER 'B17', this one being No 61663.* **Author**

downwards thereto; they are therefore 'L'-shaped and surprisingly heavy.

The 'B1' plates are straight; the antelope names have 4½in lettering, the longer director names have 3in lettering; and while the names generally are not seductive, the plates are very handsome and polish up well. The straight 'K4' and 'V4' come in the same category, splendid names but hard to find.

Some collectors like to go for the painted names on splashers. Not many of these survive and a lump of flame-cut steel is not to everyone's taste, but they deserve a mention in passing.

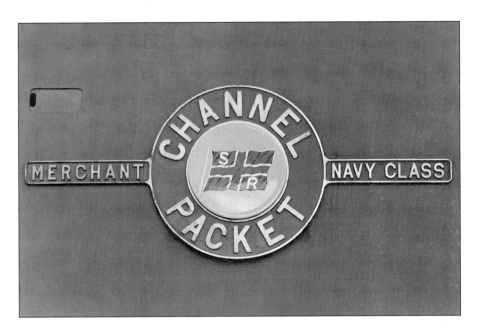

## Southern

There is a fair variety here, with the prestigious 'Merchant Navy' class heading the list. Again, these are much larger and heavier than you might suppose. They are in four parts: the centre plaque with the flag (which flies towards the rear of the locomotive, so you can always tell left from right), the surrounding circle giving the name of the shipping line, and the thinner wings reading 'Merchant . . . Navy Class'. These are gunmetal, not brass, and do not hold a decent polish. The enamel centres took a fearful bashing and it is rare to find an undamaged one.

'West Country' nameplates and scrolls are also gunmetal and the crest (if carried) has an elegant shield surround. Again, the crests suffered damage easily. 'Battle of Britain' nameplates are gunmetal and elegant; the oval shield may contain a plain RAF crest or individual squadron badge. Some of those named after individuals may have the family coat of arms if one had been granted, otherwise a plain RAF crest.

All of these are well sought after and

command heavy money; the few 'West Country' names without shields are cheaper (relatively speaking). There are a lot of replica scrolls around but nobody seems to mind too much.

The 'Lord Nelson', 'Schools' and 'Remembrance' plates are heavy lumps and the castings are rough, with sandholes visible. When sold, many were put through a milling machine to try to improve things, not always with success. The straight 'King Arthur' and Isle of Wight 'O2' plates are a bit better made, and popular because of their smaller size. The curved Brighton Atlantic plates are also popular, and mainly good names, although *Selsey Bill* and *Portland Bill* always sound like a pair of burglars.

**Above:** *The 'complete set' on the side of SR unrebuilt Bulleid Pacific No 34054. The badge and plate together are most desirable and make a particularly valuable combination.*
**M. J. Robertson/Author's Collection**

**Below:** *'Schools' class No 30928* Stowe, *showing the rough casting.* **Ian Allan Library**

**Above:** *Rebuilt 'Battle of Britain' class No 34090 Sir Eustace Missenden, Southern Railway showing the curved-style two-part nameplate and coat of arms.* **Ian Allan Library**

## British Rail

'Britannia' and 'Clan' nameplates are always popular and prices have recently shot up into five figures, a far cry from my £57 10s in the 1960s. Because they bolt through from the back, they look very well, although sometimes the weight can cause hollowing at the corners. *The Territorial Army 1908-1958*, the only double-line one, is aluminium; the weight of a brass one would probably have caused the deflectors to crumple under the strain.

The Standard Class 5 nameplates are good names but horrible castings, and there are many replicas about. Because they lasted to the bitter end, they are popular, but do take extreme care when going after them.

When you get your plate it will be advisable to insure it and your insurance company may well be awkward about the value involved. Point out firmly that this is not like having an equivalent amount of jewellery (which would go into a pocket) – stealing a 'Duchess' wants three men and a lorry and, once it reappears on the market, everyone will know whence it has come. I have never made any secret of what plates I have and if one was nicked, I am sure it would be referred straight back; secrecy *aids* the thief. As stated above, Ian Wright knows where most plates are; tell *him* what you are doing.

Ian has gone into print advocating that plates be left alone, not restored. He holds the view that original muck, bumps and scars confirm authenticity. Ian is not married. For those of us that are, and want to remain so, Management will generally agree that a beautifully polished plate may be displayed anywhere within the house, and the pleasure to be gained from this is, in my view, worth far more than the thoughts of 'How can I convince anyone this is the Real McCoy?' If you *do* restore a plate, never touch the back; what the wife don't see, the heart don't grieve over.

17

**Above:** *Nameplate seen in place on the running plate of SR 'King Arthur' No 30770* Sir Prianius. *Note the small class identification under the name. It will be appreciated how such a position for a nameplate led to 'fair wear and tear' which a potential buyer should look for and be suspicious of a mint example!*
**The Gresley Society/Author's collection**

To me, the collecting of railwayana (of which the nameplates form the major part) has been a labour of love. Mine is a small collection of less than a dozen plates but I have owned many more over the years, seeking to improve the quality of the classes (and the names). The ambition has been to get plates from locomotives that I knew, had travelled behind, illicitly driven and fired; the really personal feeling. The memories of good trips, rotten ones, finding the last of the class to complete the list in the *ABC* (what a coincidence — *Duchess of Devonshire* at £34,200 was my last 'Duchess' to underline): all those idiotic things which make non-collectors despair of understanding why anyone collects anything. Ignore them; a house without something personal is just a house, not a home.

Above all, do not collect as an investment. If you have been around for 30 or more years, then you have invested wonderfully well but accidentally. I have never thought and will never think of my collection of plates as an investment they are

gleaming old friends polished lovingly as a tribute to the craftsmen who cast them so long ago, reminders of my childhood when I first met the oldest of them. Just two I never saw, *Lady of Shalott* was scrapped two months before I was born, but the poem was part of the English Literature paper in the Oxford School Certificate exams of 1947 (passed to get back my precious *ABCs*). My LNWR plate *Goliath* is dated March 1900, for LNWR plates were both nameplates and rudimentary worksplates (without Works numbers) but the style came through from the dawn of railways: a thin brass strip, with the letters pressed into the metal, then filled with stopper, then painted black and rubbed down flat. Certainly this style was around in 1847 and was used until 1923. Curved plates had a full stop, straight ones did not, an odd quirk of a very individual railway. *Goliath* was scrapped in the month I was born; I got it as a straight swap for a 'Grange' front number plate, 6850. The name dated back to the dawn of railways, the style showed the continuity that was so much a part of railway history and which is being jettisoned everywhere today. Collect with love and you will be richly rewarded.

*Footnote:* Since this article was written, a 'King' nameplate has topped £40,000. Where will it all end?

**Above:** *Although LNWR No 790 Hardwicke was built in 1873, the LNWR followed this style of thin brass nameplate on which the letters were engraved and filled in with black, until its demise in 1923.*
**J. H. Cooper-Smith**

# CHAPTER 2

# SIGNALLING EQUIPMENT AND ASSOCIATED ITEMS

by Michael A. Vanns

Expressed very simply, there are two classes of signalling railwayana – inside equipment and outside equipment. The former comes primarily from signalboxes, although you can occasionally acquire items from ground frame cabins, crossing keepers' huts, control rooms, etc. Outside equipment is basically everything else – everything from telegraph wire insulators and point rodding compensators to signals, both semaphores and colour-lights. If you are lucky and have both the space and local authority planning permission, not to mention family tolerance, all this hardware can come together to re-create fully equipped signalboxes. All over the country there are garden signalboxes and ground frame huts in among the suburban shrubbery, with a working semaphore not far away. Personally, as long as there are not too many signals sprouting all over the place, I have always warmed more to gardens and sheds full of signalling equipment than plots of freshly painted cast-iron signs.

## Indoor Equipment

My enthusiasm for signalling started with signalbox visits. Consequently, I have always taken more of an interest in this aspect of signalling than any other. The interior of a mechanical signalbox, the atmosphere, the sounds and smells, are very special. When I started collecting, it was important to me

that the items retained that magic, that they were in 'ex-box condition'. This was, and still is, far more important to me than monetary value. Unfortunately, at one time there was so much signalbox equipment on the market that many collectors (and dealers) had no qualms about stripping off the old paint or the distressed French polish, in order to 'restore' the item (with best Dulux and polyurethane) to what they believed was 'original' condition. That belief was, of course, completely misfounded. You cannot turn back the clock. The history of an item is as much a part of its final railway condition as the long-since vanished pristine state in which it left the factory. For me, the marks of usage — flaking paint, wood bleached by the sun or polished thin because it was adjacent to brass fittings, wood worn away by the countless strikes of signalmen's hands and fingers, the accumulation of grease and dirt – are as important as any 'patina' on a piece of 18th century furniture. For me, a block instrument polyurethaned by an enthusiast is dead and without provenance.

As the price and value of signalbox equipment has increased over the years, there is fortunately less of this sort of enthusiast 'restoration' work being carried out. The problem now is not the rescue of items before the paint stripper comes into play, but the inflated prices being asked for genuinely

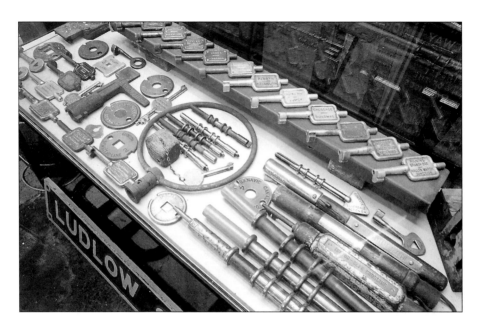

tatty items. There are still a few collectors who fall into the trap of assuming a particular piece of equipment has a particular price. Currently, because auctions are the main means of dealing in railwayana, you will hear people quoting auction prices when a similar item appears for sale elsewhere. 'A "Midland pegger" fetched £X at Y,' they will say. A 'Midland pegger' marked and dated with original plates attached, known provenance, good ex-box condition, fully working, should never be the same price as one with 'false' plates attached, unknown provenance, immaculate polyurethaned finish but broken single needle unit.

Having said that, some collectors are prepared to pay inflated prices because an instrument has a particular plate. A few years ago a number of SR Standard three-position block instruments with 'original' enamel plates were auctioned for twice the price of identical instruments without them. Not only was the plate in effect costing the equivalent of a complete instrument but those instruments without plates were sometimes in better overall condition. Given the added

**Above:** *A selection of single line tablets, key tokens and staffs. The three staffs in the foreground on the right are Webb & Thompson examples, with three wooden staffs for 'staff and ticket' working behind. In the middle of the showcase is a hoop that was attached to the end of a train staff, so that it could be dispatched while the train was on the move, and within the hoop are displayed five miniature electric train staffs. The circular discs are all from Tyer's tablet instruments, while arranged along the back of the case are 12 key tokens. **Author***

**Next page:** *Single line instruments on display at the Kidderminster Railway Museum. From left to right: Webb & Thompson's electric train staff; miniature version of the same instrument; Tyer's No 6 tablet machine; Tyer's No 7 tablet machine. Above are signalbox plates and a fine variety of signalpost finials. **Author***

23

value named plates give to an item, there is also the danger of plates (either genuine or replica) being attached by dealers just to increase the price.

While discussing plates, it is appropriate here to mention 'shelf' and lever plates. The former embraces both those once genuinely attached to block shelves and those which were affixed directly to instruments. Lever plates range from hand-engraved brass examples to more modern ones machine-engraved on 'Traffolite'. The price of these items incorporating a place name has increased enormously in the past few years. Age seems to be of no consequence, price apparently entirely dependent on the name. A well-polished, hand-chiselled number from an early Saxby & Farmer lever frame will still not command the price of a machine-engraved BR(WR) shelf plate with a name. Likewise a long ex-GWR brass lever lead with a list of numbers will fetch a hundred times more than an ex-LNER 'Traffolite' plate with an equivalent sequence of 'pulling' numbers.

The above examples indicate that collectors of railwayana are prepared to pay for memories rather than history. But in our 'heritage' world, price is often used as an indication of rarity and importance. It is assumed that the higher the price, the rarer the piece. But price and value are not the same thing, and monetary worth should not be confused with historical importance. A Reid Brothers single needle telegraph instrument is historically just as significant as a Walker's double semaphore block instrument. Modern railway signalling grew from electric telegraphy; Walker's instrument was intended to be a telegraph instrument for the illiterate. But the former might command a price of £100, whereas the latter could

**Above:** *A Tyer's co-operative permissive block instrument for recording the number of trains accepted onto a section of goods or slow line. These instruments were popular on the MS&LR, GCR and the LYR and many were marked with the companies' initials.* **Author**

approach £1,000, or even more, at auction.

Whether I like it or not, however, price and monetary value are very important to the majority of collectors. Surprisingly, how much you pay is often dependent on who is selling an item and where. For better or worse, the advent of the specialist railwayana auction has had a profound effect on prices. As with all railwayana, auctions have pushed prices upwards, and although signalling

**Previous page:** *Another view of the same display, showing a close-up of the Tyer's No 6 instrument. In the background is a Tyer's key token instrument. The semaphore arm with the 'S' is GWR vintage, used to signal 'shunt ahead' movements.* **Author**

'devices' do not consistently command the same prices as locomotive nameplates or station 'totems', certain items are now guaranteed to create a stir at certain auctions – sometimes even heart attacks! Some people would argue that auctions have made 'antiques' of many railway items, giving them a status that they did not have 20 years ago. Be that as it may, it is still possible to buy good quality signalling items other than at auctions and at less than antique prices. Putting together a collection this way is easier on the nerves, is probably more satisfying but requires a greater degree of patience than in pre-auction days.

The look of a piece of signalbox equipment will also effect its collectability and value. A cast-iron signal wire adjuster, or a signalbox stool, will be worth much less than a signal repeater with a miniature semaphore arm in a wooden case. The latter is an acceptable ornament on the mantelpiece, whereas a cast-iron wheel is certainly not female-friendly. (I have an ex-Midland Railway 12-lever frame in my front room, but then I am not married!) Any instrument incorporating miniature semaphores seems to fetch more at auctions than similar needle instruments. A Tyer's one-wire, two-position semaphore block instrument used by the LBSCR, GSWR or CR will usually fetch more than an almost identical needle instrument used by the GER. Historically, the GER variant is older and directly descended from Edward Tyer's pioneering work of the 1860s. The semaphore equivalents were produced in the 1870s as a response to railway companies who wanted an instrument with compatible indications to those on their Walker's and/or Preece equipment. Another obvious example of looks affecting price is the comparison of Great Northern Railway block bells with all other companies' examples. The former are simply not as highly prized because the bells are not visible and cannot be lovingly polished.

The varying condition and 'polishability'

of signalbox equipment, combined with the enormous variety of designs produced over the years, means that looks combined with prejudice effect the value of an item for the collector. I once knew someone who collected only LNWR signalling equipment. (Very little to polish there.) I am unusual among collectors in giving house room to a selection of BR's standard block instruments, designed by S. Williams, Signal Engineer of the London Midland Region in the middle of the 1950s and scornfully known as 'Woolworth's Block Instruments' by traditionalist signalling engineers. Dealers still have problems persuading people to buy these, because they are seen as characterless, the antithesis of a steam-worked railway. Tyer's and Sykes postwar instruments are also not yet fully appreciated, despite the fact that they were produced in far fewer numbers than their predecessors and are consequently numerically rarer.

Unlike everything mentioned so far, the signalbox diagram, a representation of the track layout with all signals and points that were controlled by the signalman clearly marked, was one of the few completely unique items inside a signalbox. These diagrams are collectable today for many reasons. For the signalling historian, they accurately show track layouts, allowing a comparison with other official records or Ordnance Survey maps, especially if they are dated. Sometimes diagrams included a representation of the interlocking of the signalbox's lever frame, and some even had the gradient profile of the section of track adjacent to the signalbox. But collectability is probably based more on purely aesthetic grounds, because many diagrams, particularly Victorian ones, were beautifully drawn and hand-coloured, making them acceptable pictures for the lounge wall.

At the other end of the scale are signalbox registers. Like diagrams they are unique records of a particular signalbox, every train and every bell code sent and

**Above:** *A Reid Brothers' single needle telegraph instrument of the 1870s in a heavy mahogany case, complete with a sloping shelf to record the messages sent and received.* **Author**

**Above:** *A close-up of the same instrument with the top removed to reveal the interior with original railway dust and rust! The needle unit is clearly marked 'Gt EASTERN RAILWAY' along with all the letters of the alphabet and their equivalent Morse codes, represented as strokes of the needle to the left or right.* **Author**

received carefully recorded by the signalmen, minute by minute, hour by hour, day by day. At first you eagerly thumb through these surviving chronicles of working life, expecting to find a catalogue of interesting incidents. But you soon learn that railway work was more often than not simply repetitive. Between a signalman signing on and off duty, the majority of entries are routine ones. There might be the occasional 'seven bells' (stop and examine), signal failure or, at weekends, an engineering possession. Of what actually happened during these 'incidents', whether it was a difficult problem, a dangerous one, or just plain routine, there is usually no comment, just a

**Right:** *The electro-magnets inside an early version of a Walker's double semaphore instrument, probably untouched since it left the manufacturer's 120 years ago. No need for 'restoration' here.* **Author**

start time and the hour and minute when it was finally sorted out. Unless they are very old or have personal associations, train registers can be very disappointing for the signalling collector. The most interesting part of a train register from a signalbox manned by my uncle are not the entries themselves, but the fact that when he was on duty, down line entries on the left-hand pages were written with his left hand and those for the up line on the right-hand pages were written with his right hand. He still has not forgiven that teacher who forced him to write with his 'wrong' hand.

All this leads on to my final observation about signalbox equipment, summed up in oneword – context. I am fortunate enough to have the space to display a number of block shelves around the house. All the shelves are the real thing (all bought for little more than the price of scrap wood) and on them I am able to assemble appropriate equipment. For such displays, the block switch and block bells are just as important as the more handsome pegging and non-pegging instruments. As another example of price bearing no relationship to historical importance or usage, the block switch from LBSCR Birchden Junction signalbox was on sale for £15 in 1985 at Collectors' Corner, whereas to obtain directly from British Rail one of the last working Tyer's one-wire, two-position semaphore block instruments from the same line five years later, collectors had to bid close to four figures. In Birchden Junction signalbox that block switch could render two Tyer's semaphore instruments completely inert!

Representative block shelves with all the associated paraphernalia are certainly more satisfying than rows of individual instruments. But the ultimate home for any signalbox equipment must be an authentic signalbox. If an analogy is needed, the comparison must be between keeping animals in a zoo as opposed to in a safari park. Neither is their natural habitat, but the latter seems more humane. Reconstructing

**Above:** *A Tyer's one-wire, two-position needle instrument as used by the GER. The design of this instrument dated back to 1869 although the 'flaps' — one obscuring the 'line clear' plunger and the other smaller one with 'TRAIN PASSED' cast in brass — were added many years later as a cheap way of making the instrument show three indications instead of two. Although the face has been re-lettered recently, the well-worn mahogany case has escaped the polyurethane treatment.*
***Author***

the whole environment of a signalbox then makes the collection of first-aid boxes, galvanised buckets, flag holders, omnibus telephones, special notices, cast-iron stoves, kettles and teapots of every shape and size legitimate and rewarding. It also means you get that lever frame out of the front room and into the place where it belongs!

28

## Outdoor Equipment

Every signalbox had at least one name board and for the signalling enthusiast these are now becoming as highly prized as totems or engine nameplates are to other collectors. The advantage of collecting signalbox boards as opposed to nameplates, however, is that the former can usually be acquired for less than the price of a small house, although GWR cast-iron examples (especially if they are unmanageably long) seem to be reaching the price of small cars.

Next to a railway and a passing train, signalboxes could look quite insignificant. But once transposed to an English country garden, even the smallest signalbox is considerably larger than the average potting shed. Despite this, and perhaps inevitably considering many Britons are genetically eccentric, there are garden signalboxes all over the country. Many hours of hard physical work are usually required before the signalling enthusiast can indulge in the ultimate satisfaction, namely 'pulling off' his very own signal from his very own lever frame.

Having observed that signalboxes are garden sheds on steroids, it has to be said that semaphore signals are also larger pieces of equipment than you first imagine. Even the smallest ground signal is usually a substantial object, most examples being made predominantly of cast iron. The shortest posts for running signals (home or distant) are seldom less than 10ft high and this excludes any below-ground section. It takes a brave collector to raise a tall timber post, which might be a foot square at the base and need a hole 5ft deep, in his garden. Signal arms also range in size from the manageable to monsters such as the GWR's late Victorian/early Edwardian 5ft long versions. Of the thousands of signals and hundreds of varieties that were in use on every railway company the length and breadth of the country barely 50 years ago, it is not surprising that a good selection of pre-Grouping arms, fittings and often whole posts survive.

**Above:** *A Fletcher's combined signal arm and lamp repeater manufactured in the LNWR's Crewe Signal Department. If the signal had not responded correctly to the signalman's pull, the circular opening to the right of the miniature semaphore displayed a small disc lettered 'WRONG'. If the light in the signal lamp was extinguished, the disc below the miniature semaphore lettered 'IN' dropped away to reveal the word 'OUT'.* **Author**

Colour-light signals are not as popular as semaphores but they too will have their day alongside British Rail's 'plastic blocks' mentioned above. 'Searchlight' signals are now very rare animals and worthy of preservation.

Obviously, not everyone has room for a

**Above:** *A GWR signalbox at the bottom of the garden. Seen in 1997.* **Chris Pratt**

whole signal, and, reminiscent of the British 'trophy' hunters during their safaris in India, Africa and Australia, many collectors of outdoor signalling equipment still tend to focus only on bits of their quarry. Signal arms are quite satisfying on their own but what remains a favourite target is the finial on top of a signal post. This has become the equivalent of the rhinoceros horn in the trophy room. Every railway company and signalling contractor produced its own styles, most cast in iron, and for those collectors brought up on the caustic dip or the sand-blaster there is nothing better to strip down, repaint in brilliant white and display like antlers, than a variety of cast-iron finials. As with most Victorian metalwork, the quality of design is invariably matched by the quality of the casting.

## A Few Thoughts

Signalling is still a specialist interest among railway enthusiasts. Whereas a cast-iron sign, locomotive nameplate, totem, lamp or more obvious items such as crested crockery are all readily understood and appreciated, a Tyer's polarised relay is not something everyone can immediately warm to. As I mentioned above, signalling equipment really needs to be appreciated in context, and far fewer enthusiasts have experienced the workings of a signalbox than have watched trains go by. As with all 'collectables', much of the appeal of the item is the memories it conjures up in the imagination of the collector. With traditional signalling being rapidly confined to preserved railways, will the appeal of collecting signalling equipment

**Above:** *Two immaculately restored ex-GWR wooden semaphores at Fencote station.* **Author**

diminish over the years, as less people like myself remember the tinkling of a single needle telegraph instrument, or the distinctive sound of a Sykes 'lock and block' instrument being operated?

As with much Victorian technology, signalling equipment was created, perfected, mass-produced and became redundant in a comparatively short space of time. Traditional antiques usually have longer pedigrees. Furniture, jewellery, costumes, paintings, etc all have a long history, and will continue to be made, collected and understood because of their associations with everyday life as it will undoubtedly continue to be lived in the future. The world of work,

particularly manual labour, however, has changed so much already that many people will have had no practical experience of, for example, a simple lever. But perhaps the appeal of signalling equipment will outlive personal memories as perceptions of the objects change. Perhaps block instruments will become the 'poor man's' scientific instruments of the future — as much 'curiosities' divorced from their original function and the society that produced them as 18th century brass microscopes are for today's collector? Quite what will happen to all those garden signalboxes and signals when their owners are dead, however, is another question.

**Above:** *Just four of the many signalbox name boards on show at the Kidderminster Railway Museum.* **Author**

**Above:** *One of the longer cast-iron GWR signalbox name boards, with a selection of signal finials displayed above.* **Author**

**Above:** *The MS&LR appears to have put a few single-needle units in 'gothic-style' cases like this one, probably from a crossing keeper's cabin. The case is not marked with either the manufacturer's or the user's name or initials, and only the single needle unit is stamped 'Spagnoletti & Crookes'. The paper face is a typical LNER or BR(E) modification.* **Author**

**Above:** *A sight to make any signalling enthusiast envious – four different types of 'train describers' at the Kidderminster Railway Museum. More accurately they ought to be called routeing instruments because they describe the destination of trains rather than the trains themselves. In the foreground are three Fletcher's describers as manufactured by and used on the LNWR, with an SR 'magazine' describer on the extreme right. Behind from left to right is a 24-description Walker's receiving instrument, a Tyer's 16-position combined sending and receiving describer, a Walker's 12-description receiving instrument with bell, and a Walker's 24-description sending instrument. These instruments are never easy to describe!* **Author**

**Above:** *An example of just one of the comparatively rare post-World War 2 double line absolute block instruments. This one is a Tyer's Type 'F', used on ex-LNER lines in Scotland. For some signalling collectors this is the instrument equivalent of a diesel.* **Author**

**Above:** *At first sight this appears to be a standard (and common) LNWR double line absolute block instrument. But the case is in fact smaller than what later became 'standard'. This particular example (No 773) was manufactured at the Stockport Signal Department in the 1890s, before the size of the case was changed. Later, this particular instrument was refurbished by the LMS, the tapper repositioned and a new base fitted with four tubular legs. Although this means it is no longer in 'original' condition, it is certainly in ex-railway condition and of considerable interest.* **Author**

**Left:** *Two examples of BR's modular 'plastic blocks', the one on the right for double lines controlled by absolute block working, the one on the left for permissive lines. These instruments were also made to indicate 'line clear' with the needle pointing to the left, and 'train on line' with the needle pointing to the right. These instruments were sometimes scathingly referred to as 'Woolworth's Block' by S&T engineers!* **Author**

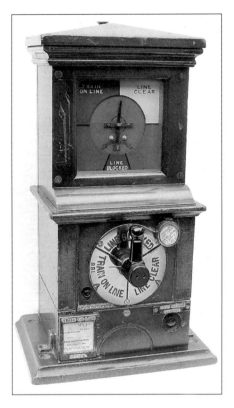

**Left:** *One of the MR's unique 'Rotary Interlocking Block Instruments'. Most of the instruments that survive in collectors' hands are marked with the company's initials and the date 1913. Other dates are rarer and worth keeping an eye out for.*
**Author**

**Below:** *A typical MR block shelf from a signalbox controlling a double line by the absolute block system. Only the block switch between the 'Rotary Block' and the ordinary 'pegger' is out of place, being of GNR vintage.* **Author**

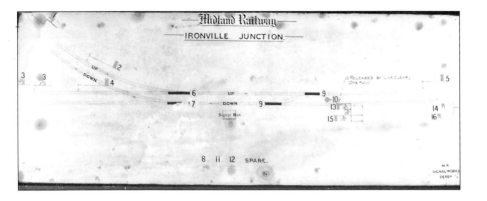

**Above:** *The MR diagram from Ironville Junction, dated September 1902.* **Author**

**Left:** *A 10-lever Dutton frame on display at the Kidderminster Railway Museum. This particular example was used by the Highland Railway.* **Author**

**Above:** *The fully operational vertical tappet locking beneath the 23 levers of a GWR frame in another 'garden' signalbox. For signalling enthusiasts this is the equivalent of looking at Walschaert's locomotive valve gear and discussing the subtleties of steam cut-offs. Interlocking is far more interesting!* **Author**

**Above:** *Cast-iron weights such as this one were often attached at the base of levers to counter-balance the length of wire between the lever and the piece of equipment it operated, if that was some distance from the signalbox. This example has clearly been manufactured by Saxby & Farmer.* **Author**

**Right:** *Each lever in an interlocking frame had its number either painted on or marked on a cast-iron, brass, or later a plastic plate which was attached to it. Illustrated here are five brass lever 'leads' — Nos 18, 19, 20 and 21 from an MR lever frame and No 105 from a GWR signalbox. The numbers beneath the lever numbers indicate which other levers have to be reversed (pulled towards the signalman) before that particular lever can be operated.* **Author**

**Above:** *On early lever frames, the number and description of what the lever operated were usually separated. Here are four MR description plates. At first the MR attached long brass plates to the right-hand side of the levers themselves, the one in the foreground here being a later example of this design. The other plates shown are examples of the later practice of positioning the descriptions behind the levers.* **Author**

**Right:** *This is a fragment from the brass description plate which should have been positioned behind the levers of Saxby & Farmer's frame No 1846. The plate was probably a reject, because this side shows no signs of polishing whereas the back is highly polished, indicating it must have spent most of its working life that way up, being used for other than its original purpose. It was bought in an antique centre for £3, labelled as 'a piece of brass'.* **Author**

**Below:** *The LNER and BR(E) continued the ex-GNR practice of large cast-iron lever plates with included both the number and description. These BR(E) examples made from 'Traffolite' (which would have been attached to the front of cast-iron plates), came from Rectory Junction at the eastern end of Colwick Yard, Nottingham.* **Author**

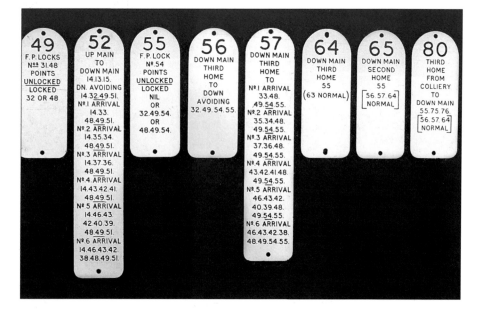

**Right**: *A bell plunger manufactured by the Sykes Interlocking Signal Co with a hand-engraved brass plate lettered WEST NORWOOD JUNCTION. The SR favoured enamelled description plates, two of which are pictured here. Plungers like this example were used to transmit bell codes between signalboxes. Some can still be found in service; others are fetching surprising prices for what were recently being thrown away.* **Author**

**Right**: *If signalboxes were close together, the operation of stop signals might be so arranged that they were worked from more than one box. Such signals were called 'slotted' signals. A similar 'slotting' arrangement was used when the distant signal of one box was positioned under the stop signal of the signalbox in rear of it. The ex-GNR cast-iron 'slot' indicator shown here was a means of telling a signalman whether his colleague in the adjacent box had cleared his signal, which would change the indication from 'LOCKED' to 'CLEAR'.* **Author**

41

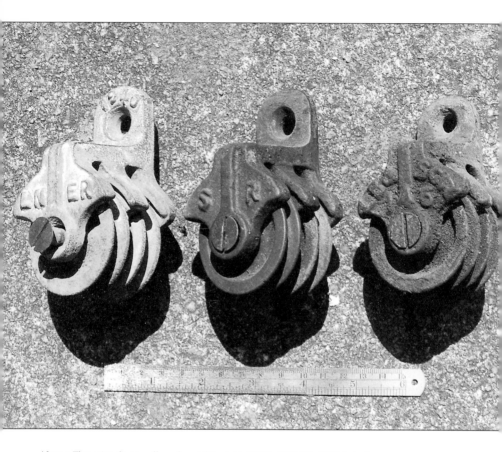

**Above:** *Three signal wire pulleys; from left to right: LNER, 1940; SR; LBSCR.* **Author**

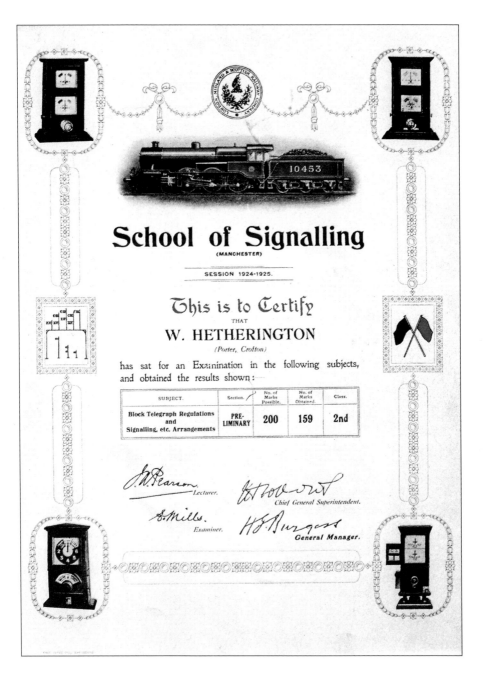

# School of Signalling

(MANCHESTER)

SESSION 1924-1925.

## This is to Certify

THAT

### W. HETHERINGTON

*(Porter, Crofton)*

has sat for an Examination in the following subjects, and obtained the results shown:—

| SUBJECT. | Section. | No. of Marks Possible. | No. of Marks Obtained. | Class. |
|---|---|---|---|---|
| Block Telegraph Regulations and Signalling, etc. Arrangements | PRE-LIMINARY | 200 | 159 | 2nd |

*J. W. Pearson.*
Lecturer.

*Chief General Superintendent.*

*S. Mills.*
Examiner.

*H. G. Burgess*
General Manager.

**Above:** *The chromo-lithographed certificate presented to W. Hetherington, who had attended the ex-LYR's Signalling School at Manchester in 1924/5 and was awarded a Second Class for his 'Block Telegraph Regulations and Signalling, etc. Arrangements'.* **Author**

# CHAPTER 3

# CAST-IRON SIGNS

## by John Mander

Steam had gone, it seemed for ever. The gods with whom our impressionable youth had been spent had been riven from us and lay rusting or cut in pieces and part of the world we had built was shattered. It was the 1970s and what could we replace them with?

Some of us began to wander along lifted trackbeds, abandoned lines, or those with a possible train a day, and there along the linesides lived cast-iron notices. By some happy coincidence, some of the earliest lines to be abandoned — and thus easy to walk upon usually totally undisturbed for days on end — harboured notices so arcane that we had to make a note and return home to learn what they stood for. Working out the initials 'S. Y. J. L. C.' (South Yorkshire Joint Line Committee) was a little difficult, especially if one did not know the line to have belonged jointly to the Lancashire & Yorkshire, North Eastern, Midland, Great Northern and Great Central Railways! Another one was the 'W. M. & C. Q. R.', whose signs were advertised only thus; to make matters worse, the GCR had erased one of the letters, to make the characters more like 'GCR'! This turned out to be the Wrexham, Mold & Connah's Quay Railway.

The excitement of such discoveries began to assuage the blankness caused by the

*Below: A wall at the author's one-time Moseley Railway Museum, with signs from, among others, Leeds High Level, Carlisle Citadel Station Committee, Halifax High Level, West London Joint, London & Birmingham et al.* **John Mander**

**Above:** *The 'Great Northern Zone' in snow at the former Moseley Railway Museum. On the central post are two trespass notices, a weak bridge notice, bridge and viaduct numbers, with a GN & LNW Joint gate sign to the left and two other bridge signs to the right. Thoughtfully displayed like this, a collection of signs can be a characterful addition to a garden.* **John Mander**

end of steam. It is worth prefacing a very general view of cast-iron signs with these visions of excitement, which quickly turned into a national treasure hunt.

## Bridge Plates

It took only a short period for the most lucrative locations to become apparent. Bridges on almost all lines had bridge plates, the Great Western being one exception to prove a rule. It was usual for double track lines to have one facing each way, giving at least two per bridge, while single lines usually sported one only. They were often secured by spikes driven into the mortar, which had frequently rusted away, leaving the plate loose or even fallen down and buried in ballast or vegetation. On the parapets were often 'spiked in' warning notices regarding vehicles prohibited from

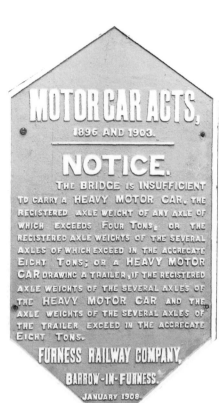

*Right: This hexagonal notice fascinates due to the perfectly balanced layout with six letter sizes, plus the full company name, address and date.*
**John Mander**

*Below: The style of bridge plate used on the Cockermouth, Keswick & Penrith Railway was unique to the line. A remarkable number have survived.* **Henry Noon**

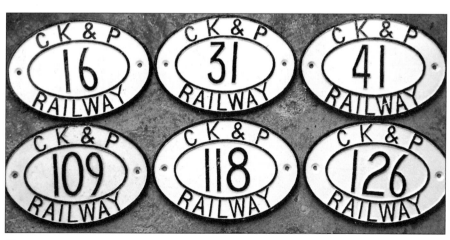

passing over. Usually these were two per bridge, sometimes aided and abetted by huge diamond signs, one at each end of the bridge.

There were occasional bonanzas for collectors. On the Rhymney Railway bridges could be found a pair of small diamonds on posts plus two rectangles on the parapets, not to mention named bridge numbers on the arches underneath.

Besides ultra-common lines such as the London & North Western (and its type-successors LMS and BR), Great Eastern and North Eastern Railways, there was every graduation of variety through to almost impossible rarities, like the West London, Carlisle Citadel, Wakefield Joint, LNW & Furness Joint, and – most improbable of all – LNW & Midland Joint.

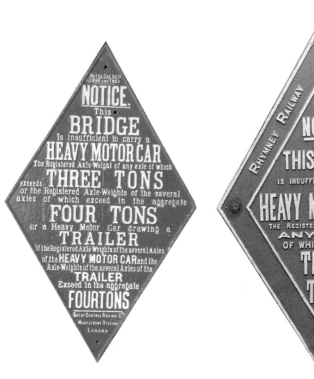

MOTOR CAR ACTS
1896 AND 1903
**NOTICE.**
This
**BRIDGE**
is insufficient to carry a
**HEAVY MOTOR CAR**
The Registered Axle-Weight of any axle of which
exceeds **THREE TONS**
or the Registered Axle-Weights of the several
axles of which exceed in the aggregate
**FOUR TONS**
or a Heavy Motor Car drawing a
**TRAILER**
if the Registered Axle-Weights of the several Axles
of the **HEAVY MOTOR CAR** and the
Axle-Weights of the several Axles of the
**TRAILER**
Exceed in the aggregate
**FOUR TONS**
GREAT CENTRAL RAILWAY C.º
MARYLEBONE STATION
LONDON

RHYMNEY RAILWAY COMPANY.
**NOTICE.**
**THIS BRIDGE**
IS INSUFFICIENT TO CARRY
**HEAVY MOTOR CARS**
THE REGISTERED AXLE WEIGHT OF
**ANY AXLE**
OF WHICH EXCEEDS
**THREE TONS**

**MIDLAND RAILWAY.**
7 VICT. CAP. 18.5 EC. 238 ENACTS "THAT IF ANY
PERSON SHALL BE OR TRAVEL OR PASS UPON FOOT
UPON THE MIDLAND RAILWAY WITHOUT THE
LICENSE AND CONSENT OF THE MIDLAND RAILWAY
COMPANY, EVERY PERSON SO OFFENDING SHALL
FORFEIT AND PAY ANY SUM NOT EXCEEDING TEN
POUNDS FOR EVERY SUCH OFFENCE."
NOTICE IS THEREFORE HEREBY GIVEN, THAT ALL
PERSONS FOUND TRESPASSING UPON THIS RAILWAY
OR THE WORKS THEREOF WILL BE PROSECUTED.
JAMES WILLIAMS.
JUNE 1893. SECRETARY.

**Above:** *Two diamond bridge notices. The GCR one (left) is of the standard design and refers to the 1896 and 1903 Motor Car Acts. The Rhymney Railway example is infinitely more desirable, with the company name in the border, a less cluttered design and several attractive lettering styles.* **John Mander**

**Left:** *The standard Midland Railway weak bridge sign; this one is dated 1893 and records James Williams as the company secretary.* **John Mander**

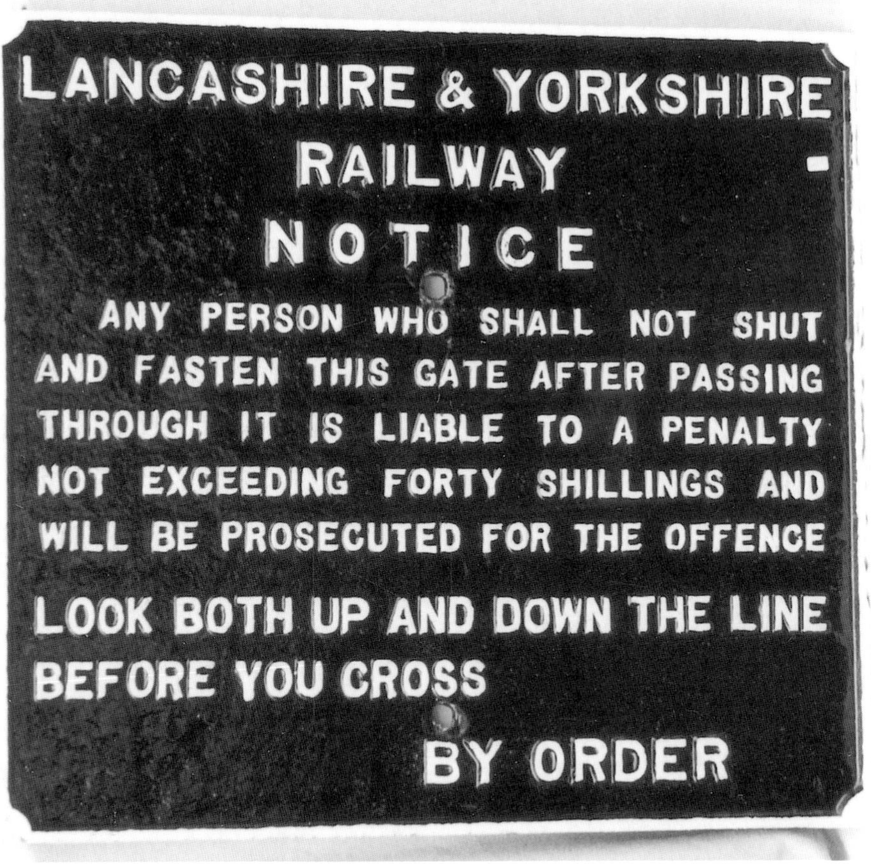

LANCASHIRE & YORKSHIRE
RAILWAY
NOTICE
ANY PERSON WHO SHALL NOT SHUT
AND FASTEN THIS GATE AFTER PASSING
THROUGH IT IS LIABLE TO A PENALTY
NOT EXCEEDING FORTY SHILLINGS AND
WILL BE PROSECUTED FOR THE OFFENCE

LOOK BOTH UP AND DOWN THE LINE
BEFORE YOU CROSS
                              BY ORDER

## Gate Signs

Gate signs were divided into footpaths, farm accommodation crossings, private crossings, and, of course, level crossings. There were few lines which had not provided warnings regarding the likelihood of trains and the signs stated penalties for leaving gates open. They ranged from the simple 'Beware of Trains' to almost every size and shape, some with the mere three words, 'Shut This Gate', through to whole intricate paragraphs as with the LNWR. A small number were in Welsh only. The longest in length were the round-ended Great Northern ones, copied by the London & North Eastern, advising a 40s fine. The NER ones were in two parts and have

**Above:** *An extremely popular notice combining the demand to shut and fasten with a 40s fine warning and a reminder to look both ways.*
**John Mander**

survived in large numbers.

The great majority were in cast iron, with surprising exceptions found in enamel. In the cases of the GWR, LNWR and LNWR & GW Joint, among others, a basic framework of wooden struts was made so that the sign would fit onto the bars of the gate. Gate notices were sometimes placed on the public side, to be read before crossing. On various well-stocked lines it was possible to predict

49

**Above:** *Examples of gate signs at the former Moseley Railway Museum. From the top: LYR, LNER, MSL, MR, HBR, NER, MSL and LYR examples.* **John Mander**

**Below:** *A standard GWR full-titled gate notice.* **John Mander**

GREAT WESTERN RAILWAY.
NOTICE.
BY 8 VIC. CAP. 20. S. 75. ANY PERSON NOT FASTENING THIS GATE AFTER HAVING PASSED THROUGH IS LIABLE TO A PENALTY OF FORTY SHILLINGS.

**Below:** *Not all signs carried the company name. This is from the Cambrian Railways.* **John Mander**

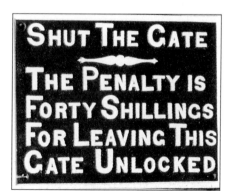

SHUT THE GATE
THE PENALTY IS
FORTY SHILLINGS
FOR LEAVING THIS
GATE UNLOCKED

**GREAT NORTHERN**
**— RAILWAY —**
**THE PUBLIC MUST NOT CROSS**
**THE LINE ON THE LEVEL BUT**
**BY THE BRIDGE.**
**BY ORDER**

exactly where signs would be found from a study of footpaths and farm crossings shown on an Ordnance Survey map. It was normal but not invariable for each crossing to have two notices, though it should be stressed that every railway had its own pattern of locations. Stile crossings on the GNR had small numbered ovals without words.

*Above: The GNR made large numbers of signs in this style, but only two or three are known which carry this message. **John Mander***

### Trespass Plates

Trespass plates are some of the most sought-after items and one famous collector acquires these only as his speciality. Wording varies from the most basic 'Trespassers Will be Prosecuted', as given on the London & South Western, some early LNWR plates and the

*Below: The Truro-Penzance West Cornwall Railway was provided with GWR-style gate notices (unless the GWR copied the WCR!). Only some 13 survive at the most. **John Mander***

**WEST CORNWALL RAILWAY**
**BY 8 VIC.CAP.20.S.75. ANY PERSON NOT**
**FASTENING THIS GATE AFTER HAVING**
**PASSED THROUGH IS LIABLE TO A PENALTY**
**OF FORTY SHILLINGS.**

Taff Vale Railway, through to densely packed lines of writing. This was due to some companies being advised to cite the relevant Act of Parliament with attendant verbiage, while others favoured a simple sign in large letters. Some of these plates are fairly small and light, such as the short LNWR version, whereas others were vast and ponderous, of which the standard Midland and NER ones were and are notorious.

Besides the style of lettering and the size and layout of each plate, a most important matter for collectors is whether initials only or full company titles were used. Long joint companies sometimes had to use abbreviations like 'Met. and Gt. Central Joint', or 'GW & GC Joint Committee', which are inferior to a full title such as

*Left: Two Southern Railway signs, both referring to the SR Act of 1924: the top one is in LSWR style and the lower is the new standard SR style.*
**John Mander**

**Left:** *Just before the opening of the last century, in January 1899, this large and rare trespass plate was erected at a company reservoir.* **John Mander**

**Above:** *An amazing sign, relating to the station and goods lines at Carlisle Citadel. Note the two full titles. This ranks second in the top 100 signs of 1985-99 (see page 59).* **John Mander**

(see page 59)

'Cockermouth, Keswick & Penrith Railway', of which only two examples are known. A few cases exist where an absorbed line has its title after that of its owner. An excellent family of cases is the 'Midland Railway L. T. & S. Section' and 'LNWR & GW Joint Lines Vale of Towy Railway'. On the whole, trespass plates are the most valued of all cast-iron signs.

## Boundary Posts

Boundary posts have been found, sometimes in profusion. They can be warmly recommended as meaningful adornments to gardens, occupying little space when restored and dug in. Some are very small and almost dainty, as with GNR and LSWR examples,

**Above:** *The Midland & Great Northern Joint had signs in Midland, in GNR and later in LNER style. This is a GNR-style example.* **John Mander**

**Left:** *A '40/-' GCR trespass sign. This line had a large number of variations in the style of these signs.* **John Mander**

**Left:** *A Somerset & Dorset Joint trespass sign, produced in LSWR style, dated 5 August 1903, with the names of the Joint Secretaries.* **John Mander**

54

the former only some 4ft high and slender. The most common are still available today at as little as £30 to £50. Company initials and sometimes a full name are embossed or inscribed into the sides, or, rarely, in a garter on the top. They came in many styles, ranging from the early ones in the shape of the road mileposts of the mid-19th century, right through to the BR adaptation of the GWR type. An uncommon 'British Railways Western Region' was cast in the exact style of the ubiquitous GWR version.

Locations varied according to the company. The GNR favoured field boundaries in corners, especially where little rivulets flowed under their lines; the LNWR often put whole lines of boundary posts in, sometimes being found hundreds of yards away from the actual line, where land had been bought and not used or where a dispute had occurred. I remember the ultimate excitement of finding three Brecon & Merthyr posts marked 'B&MR' lying already pulled up in a ditch near Brecon. They remain, to this day, the only ones known to survive.

Another startling find was a whole curve full to bursting with 'N. W. & L. R.' posts (North Wales & Liverpool Railway), which later became part of the GCR empire. They were every 30 yards or so, in totally regular spacing. At that time no one had any inkling that such artefacts existed, so finding them was akin to the recent relocation of a sunken Roman battle fleet — at least if you are a collector of cast-iron.

**Above:** *A Weymouth Joint Line boundary post, in GWR style, relocated into a daffodil bed.*
**Rodney Marshall**

### Goods Offices and Depots
Another lucrative area consisted of goods offices and depots, which were often festooned with signs reading 'No Locomotives to Enter', 'Mechanical Capstans', 'No Smoking', and a legion of others. The most prolific was the LYR, which spawned a whole family of signs. Entrances with weighbridges were often adorned and the NER had one specifying times when the depot was open. Notable and highly valued signs were found on GWR joint lines, especially GW & GC Joint and GW & LNW Joint.

**Below:** *Boundary posts of the Pontypridd, Caerphilly & Newport (left) and Alexandra Newport Dock & Railway Co.* **John Mander**

**Above:** *A GWR triangular boundary post. These came in two variants and preceded the standard circular-topped style.* **John Mander**

## Private Paths and Private Roads

Private paths and private roads were sometimes predictable homes to signs advising the public that, welcome as they were to use the said station approach, they were visitors on sufferance only. Notable examples were made by the GWR, LSWR, South Eastern, London Chatham & Dover, LNER and many more. The GWR one was especially fine, as it had a base addition to the main sign, with a pointing finger and 'GWR Station'. In some cases the relevant Act of Parliament was cited in the notice, as with the 1924 Acts of the Southern and the LNER.

*Below: One of a large family of LYR notices about goods depot machinery.* **John Mander**

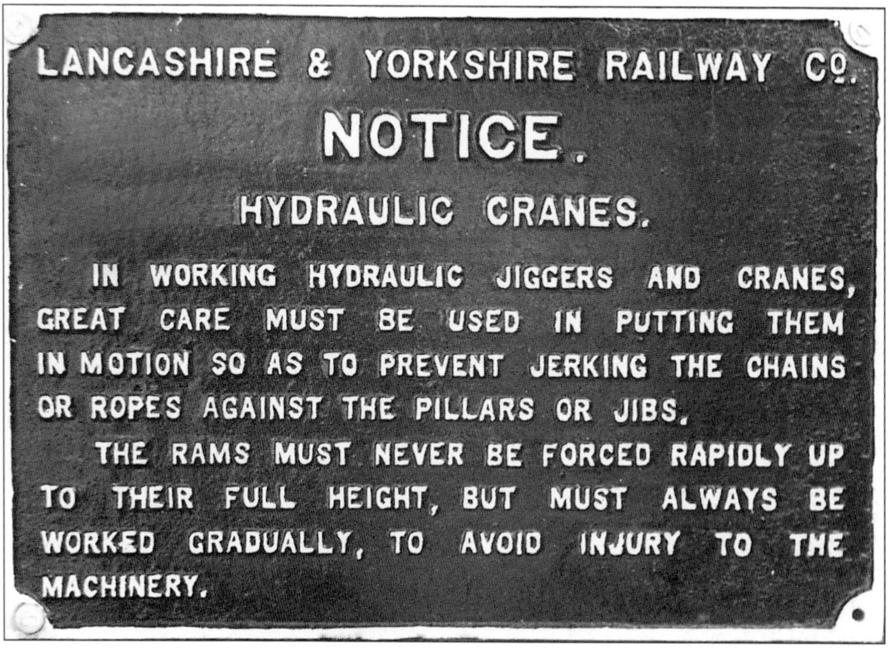

LANCASHIRE & YORKSHIRE RAILWAY C⁰.

NOTICE.

HYDRAULIC CRANES.

IN WORKING HYDRAULIC JIGGERS AND CRANES, GREAT CARE MUST BE USED IN PUTTING THEM IN MOTION SO AS TO PREVENT JERKING THE CHAINS OR ROPES AGAINST THE PILLARS OR JIBS.

THE RAMS MUST NEVER BE FORCED RAPIDLY UP TO THEIR FULL HEIGHT, BUT MUST ALWAYS BE WORKED GRADUALLY, TO AVOID INJURY TO THE MACHINERY.

L N E R NOTICE

VEHICLES MUST NOT CROSS THIS WEIGHBRIDGE EXCEPT FOR WEIGHING CARE MUST BE EXERCISED WHEN DRAWING ON AND OFF.

THE GROSS WEIGHT OF SELF-PROPELLED VEHICLES USING THIS WEIGHBRIDGE MUST NOT EXCEED 15 TONS

*Left: The LNER, like the LYR, had a large range of goods yard notices.* **John Mander**

57

**Above:** *Signs such as these were commonly bolted on company forecourts, outside stations and approach ways. Each company developed its own style.* **John Mander**

### 'No Bill Posters'

Areas adjacent to railways quite often sported 'No Bill Posters' and variants upon. The LNWR had a 'Post No Bills', the GNR had several patterns, always in very small letters, and the GCR had at least three styles.

Along the ground lay a plethora of cast-iron signs for those with eyes. The cattle markets around Kettering station were full of Midland Railway drain covers and stop valve plates, and when Swindon Works was being demolished, there were exposed rows of large covers for storm water drains, sewers and various other services. The GWR was prolific with its ground level notices, and many other companies did their own too. The Manchester, Sheffield & Lincolnshire and its successor the GCR had large numbers on their station walls. The most famous 'family' of stop valve and related signs was on the LNWR, with its round-cornered signs.

### Stations

We should not omit various other areas well supplied by some companies. Stations very commonly had 'Drinking Water' 'Not Drinking Water' signs inside WCs, while the famous GWR sign in gents' toilets, 'Please Adjust your Dress Before Leaving', caused some speculation among gentlemen collectors as to how they might get inside ladies' conveniences to see what was said there! The solution, rather than risk being caught inside, was to send your lady friend or wife in to see. The result was a great disappointment, as it appears that the GWR never had problems with their lady passengers exiting with dresses disarranged. Talking of 'In' and 'Out', the GWR booking office approach rails were fitted with these.

A very few lines fitted their platform drinking fountains with marked cast-iron notices, the North British Railway being one well-known case.

### Railway-owned Canals

Railway-owned canals were sometimes fertile areas for all sorts of signs regarding towpaths, bicycles prohibited/on sufferance only, and most commonly, bridge restrictions.

By far the most common are the extensive group from the Shropshire Union Railway & Canal Co, later LNWR then LMS owned.

### Door Plates and Seat Backs

Door plates and seat backs are both areas of intense interest. The round-cornered GNR/LNER species of door plate had a vast number of names and we have not seen all the survivors even now. Equally collectable are the right-angle-ended GWR family, subdivided into pre- and post-Grouping (1923). Seat back names of the GNR/LNER also had rounded ends and we are only now seeing the array of names which have been saved.

This can only be an introduction to a vast subject, and no mention has been made of whole areas of other cast-iron signs, once common, now symbols of a largely vanished feature of our railways. Hopefully, though, it has shown the possibilities of what there is to collect in this field of railwayana.

There is available *The Cast-iron Rarity & Price Guide*, covering every sign sold at auction in 1985-99, 158 pages with hundreds of illustrations, graphs and commentary by this author, obtainable at £6.00 from Birmingham Railway Publications, 7 Ascot Road, Moseley, Birmingham B13 9EN.

*Note:* Cast-iron signs are a major component of railwayana auctions, and are found on private sale. Readers should remember that the days of mass closures when the interest of these signs was not yet appreciated and they could be found redundant on closed lines, being thrown away as scrap or simply left around by demolition gangs, are gone; signs surviving on working railways usually still have significance and on preserved railways they count of course as part of the railways' ambience and property. However, unlikely finds can still turn up if you are lucky.

**Below:** *And where did the GWR run electric services? Answer — the Hammersmith & City Joint Line. Such signs can be a reminder of largely forgotten railway history.* **John Mander**

**Bottom:** *A very rare early Nationalisation era sign, bilingual and in GWR style.* **John Mander**

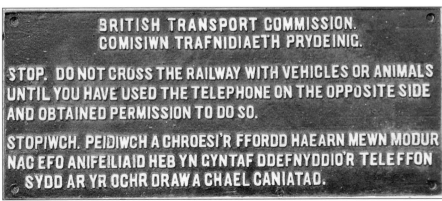

**Above:** *An example of an instruction sign. This MR example was located on a timber bridge.*
**John Mander**

*John Mander is the proprietor of Birmingham Railwayana Auctions; nine auctions are held annually, the catalogue being part of Railway Collectors' Journal, published on the first of each month (apart from January and August). Each issue cost £3.50 or six for £18, 12 for £33, from the above address. There are always cast-iron signs for sale.*

**Left:** *No one supposes that the London & Birmingham Railway had 943 or more company houses — which is where these plates came from. Presumably the first number is a district location. Such little mysteries add to the interest of a collection.* **John Mander**

# CHAPTER 4

# ENAMEL SIGNS

by Colin Tyson

The process of enamelling on to steel sheeting has proved to be one of the best mediums available for mass-produced signage for the greater part of the 20th century. Vitreous enamelling (from 'vitrify') is to form glass onto a sheet of steel at extremely high temperatures, a chemical reaction forming a bond to make the shiny, resilient, weatherproof surface. The steel sheets are pre-cut to the shape and size required, and screw holes, if needed, are added at this stage. The steel is de-greased, cleaned and etched with acid so that the first ground coat of primer (normally black) will bond. Subsequent coats using powdered glass are added, to build up the layers for fusing in a kiln at around 900° C for the first coat, to 800° C for the last.

The spread of new railway lines in the late 19th century mirrored the growth of enamel sign manufacturing, although the core sign business for enamel companies remained the production of the now highly collectable commercial advertising signs – many highly pictorial and colourful. The railways offered new prime advertising sites for commercial advertisers, and with rail connections running to many enamel factories, orders for 100,000 signs were quite normal. Porcelain enamelling on sheet iron started in Britain around 1850 and there were many companies producing at the end of the

1880s. Iron was serving many manufacturing functions and the enamel sign was an extension to the Victorian ethos of building for permanence.

The pre-Grouping railway companies around the turn of the century were not all big users of the enamel sign, for it was at the locomotive and railway workshops that cast-iron could be produced economically, with foundries casting large amounts of signage such as trackside trespass notices. With around 150 different railway concerns in existence at various times before 1923, it would be an impossible task to pick out those who used some form of enamel sign against those that most definitely did not, because of the passage of time, poor early photography and of course the fact that everyday common railway items were not always considered collectable. Pre-Grouping signage continues to surface, much to the delight of collectors and historians.

Despite the cost of enamelling over that of cast-iron, Scottish railway companies were big users. They would paint engine names directly onto locomotive splashers to save the cost of casting a nameplate, yet thought the provision of enamel trespass signs and the like to be worthwhile. The Caledonian, Great North of Scotland and North British Railways all produced fine trespass enamels, with the rarest of Scottish examples to surface thus far

**PROPPING UP OF WAGON DOORS** FOR SUPPORT OF COAL WEIGHING MACHINES OR FOR LOADING OR UNLOADING OF ANY DESCRIPTION OF TRAFFIC OR FOR ANY OTHER PURPOSE IS STRICTLY PROHIBITED. *BY ORDER OF L.B.&S C.RY C°*

being of pre-Group origin – a Dundee & Arbroath Railway trespass. Colonel Stephens, not known for his extravagance in the construction of his light railways, used enamel for his station nameboards on the Kent & East Sussex and Weston, Clevedon & Portishead railways.

One of the most popular uses of enamel signs in pre-Grouping days was for station nameboards, but not normally the large 'running-in' board types as described above. (These were often made in wood with wood or metal letters.) Small nameboards in the form of 'lamp tablets' – an enamel plate bearing the station name, curved in a horseshoe shape to fit under the contour of a lamp globe or just a simple straight bar – were quite common. Many pre-Grouping examples of these survive, with some remaining *in situ* after the Grouping. The Great Central and the Great Northern Railways favoured the horseshoe type, as later did the LNER. Image was important to the small companies and the first chance to impress was at the front of the station, with the provision of poster boards to extol the travel facilities offered. Many companies chose enamel for poster board headings and some fine examples survive, from the

*Above: A relatively early enamel sign, this one giving a clear instruction in a goods yard. This London, Brighton & South Coast sign is now on display at the Bluebell Railway (a couple of less battered examples are kept secure!).* **Author**

common South Eastern & Chatham Railway blue lettering on white long and short versions to a rare Isle of Wight Central Railway type. The London, Brighton & South Coast Railway was not known for being a large enamel user, yet produced a couple of gems none the less. A superb poster board heading with the legend 'Brighton Railway' with 'and South Coast' in a centred oval using three colours and mentioning their own marine services to the continent; and one of the finest pre-Group enamels, the sign guarding against the 'propping up of wagon doors . . .'. This seemed to be a habit for railwaymen south of the Thames, as the Southern Railway felt it necessary to produce a smaller black and white version of its own in the 1920s.

The Midland Railway and the early Great Western Railway were widespread users. The GWR produced a landscape and a portrait version of a trespass sign, with white lettering on a dark blue ground (one of the

BRITISH RAILWAYS NOTICE

WHEN THE NEIGHBOURING ROADS ARE
FLOODED PERSONS MAY PASS ON FOOT
AT THEIR OWN RISK OVER THE BRITISH
TRANSPORT COMMISSIONS STRIP OF LAND
6 FEET WIDE ON THE NORTH WEST SIDE
OF THE HEDGE FROM THE GATE TO THE STILE
TO THE FOOTPATH CROSSING THE RAILWAY.
AT OTHER TIMES THE GATE WILL BE KEPT
LOCKED BY THE PARISH COUNCIL.

BRITISH TRANSPORT COMMISSION
ESE. THE RIGHT TO TERMINATE
ARRANGEMENT WITHOUT NOTICE.

**Above:** *A remarkable survivor from early Nationalisation days, photographed some years ago, opposite to Barcombe Mills station, East Sussex, which closed in 1969. The warning of this unusually worded flood notice is obvious; like the green enamel SR sign, it has stood the test of time! Such rare or one-off signs have a special interest of their own, especially if its former location is known.* **David Mark/Author's Collection**

cheapest colours available after black). Some nicely proportioned 'named' station direction signs have survived, complete with pointing hand. Various examples of red on white titled safety notices from GWR workshops etc also survive. The commercial department produced signs, including a map of the GWR system that promoted travel by sea from Fishguard, and a highly pictorial advert depicting Cornwall as the mirror image of Italy and how they were alike in scenery and climate!

Of the 'Big Four' railways, the London, Midland & Scottish Railway produced rectangular station name lamp tablets that were black lettered on a yellow ground with a black border. Considering the many thousands that must have been made, there are relatively few survivors, station names latterly being made in cast iron, known as 'Hawkseye' target signs. The GWR continued to favour wood and cast iron, while the London & North Eastern Railway produced enamel station signage/poster board headers in white on a dark blue ground.

The Southern Railway was the biggest user of enamel at the time, complementing

64

the stark modernity of the concrete products being manufactured at its Exmouth Junction works. Most stations were supplied with enamel 'target' signs – a simple white lettering on a green bar, central within a circle. The circle remained the same size, while the amount of lettering required dictated the length of the bar. If the name was too long, or a suffix such as 'East' 'Central' 'Junction' etc was required, this would appear around the bottom of the circle. Target signs were suspended from canopies or affixed to lamp posts by means of a wooden backing board equal to the central bar and slightly angled at the top to allow rainwater to run off. These signs were produced, in the main, by Mead McLean, a London company that also made the later BR totems for a while. The SR manufactured running-in boards to fit standard size panels built into concrete platform fencing, and produced a host of miscellaneous signage with a lettering style that is discernible as being Southern when compared to the white

on green signs of the more modern Southern Region.

Not all of the Southern's signs were green and white. Early signage used blue backgrounds and black backgrounds, for example, on poster board headers. With the rolling programme of third rail electrification came red on white notices about the dangers of 'touching conductor rails', and the SR Electrical Department had some wonderful warning signs for its new installations. Two differing types of the famous Southern 'Sunshine' lettering were used, one being a rounder typeface, the other a squarer lettered style. The spread of electrification brought the opportunity to bring in new signage bearing the legend 'Southern Electric', with an electric flash running through the type. Fascia boards bearing these words were often followed by 'Fast electric trains to all parts . . .' etc.

By far the most documented and collectable era for the enamel railway sign belongs to that of the nationalised British Railways from January 1948. New signing carried the colours of the six new individual regions and a Sign Standards booklet was published in April of that year. Later, on 27 September, the Railway Executive produced a *Code of Instructions to sign manufacturers for Station Names and Direction Signs*.

This period was to be the best attempt yet at standardisation and uniformity – a new corporate image for the nation's railway, but in reality this was far from the case. Gill Sans and Gill Sans Condensed (for longer names) was chosen for a lettering style – a simple clarity that was close to styles chosen by the LNER and SR and very close to the Johnston face used very successfully by London Transport.

The colours chosen for the regions were based loosely on existing colours that were associated with the areas from both Grouped and pre-Grouping days:

**Above:** *An LBSCR poster board heading plate, which has clearly suffered in removal years ago, and a Cardiff Railway 'Smoking Prohibited' sign for use in goods yards and warehouses. Damage to an enamel sign need not destroy its value; well-meaning amateurish 'repairs' are more to be feared.* **Author**

Southern – green, virtually the same shade of dark green that the Southern Railway had used;

Western – brown, followed the GWR chocolate and cream, the BR enamels also having cream lettering;

London Midland – maroon, similar in shade to the crimson Midland Railway livery;

Scottish – light blue; a good shade of 'Caledonian' blue;

Eastern – dark blue, the same shade as LNER enamel and the GER beforehand;

North Eastern – tangerine, a choice that was an exception to the above rules! The white lettering upon this colour was not a total success, being difficult to read in bright sunlight. Later examples gave the white

**Left:** *A display of Southern Railway station target signs complement the green Southern Region totems when displayed together. This also shows how a stairwell makes an ideal display area.* **Author**

letters a black outline to overcome the problem.

A station that had been typically re-signed with the new image would start with a direction sign, double-sided and affixed by brackets to a lamp post/wall with a white BR 'totem', with the word 'STATION' and an arrow to guide you. In some cases it was thought necessary to state the station name in full; in others it was sufficient to state just 'East Station' etc if a town had more than one station. A fascia board with the legend 'British Railways' and the name of the station would greet you upon arrival.

**Right:** *Four totems (two Scottish, one LMR and one SR) on display for sale at Kidlington Railwayana Auctions.* **Author**

**Above:** *A fine front-of-station fascia board, featuring the typical blank totems. This is easily distinguished from the equally large platform running-in boards, which would only carry the station name.* **Author**

**Right:** *Enamel is universal. This Victoria Railway (Australia) example is of similar shape to the classic SR target. These signs have only recently been replaced.* **Author**

These were usually flanged at construction (ie a lip around the whole sign) to enable a wooden frame to be fixed behind and to be weatherproof. Not of a standard size because of having to be in proportion to their environment, the large nature of these signs meant that they were often produced in sections for ease of manufacture and fitting.

The message of British Railways ownership was repeated on poster board headings on station frontages – a small size for single posters (double royal size) or a longer version to fit a longer poster board (quad royal size, or two double royals!).

Some small stations had a sign that doubled up as a fascia and a poster board heading, sited perhaps at the end of the station drive. Sundry other signs could be found in the forecourt area with wording pertaining to parking/taxis/buses etc, and perhaps a door plate proclaiming 'Private' screwed to the gate of the stationmaster's house.

Once inside the booking hall, a small plate above the booking window gave notice in small print as to the 'Conditions of the Issue of Tickets' and you would be reminded at the ticket barrier to 'Please Show Tickets'.

Out on the platform, any number of a

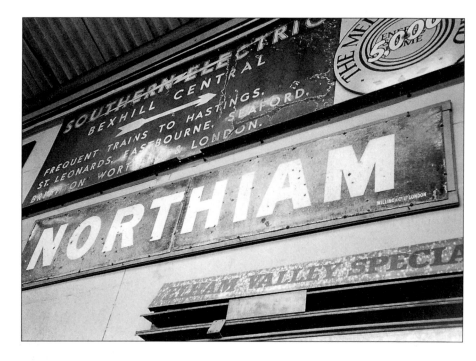

host of standard platform signs would be provided to direct you to various facilities ranging alphabetically from 'Buffet' to 'Way Out'. Together with 'Platform Number' signs, these were suspended from roofs or fixed to walls as appropriate. Signs carrying only a platform number were usually suspended nearer to the platform edge than other signs.

Door plates, frameless and either flat or with a shallow flange, were provided at eye or handle level, again in a host of titles ranging from 'Buffet' to 'Waiting Room'.

At the incoming end of the platform was the large station name sign, or running-in board, which was either flanged, frameless or flat, or framed in concrete. These sometimes gave additional wording, such as that needed for junction stations. The signalbox carried a fully flanged nameboard.

On top of all this sign activity was the provision of the ubiquitous 'totem' station sign, provided at suitable intervals along the platform on lamp standards, suspended

**Above:** *Signs on display at the Kent & East Sussex Railway, Tenterden. The early KESR 'Northiam' station enamel is marked as by Willings of London. Above, the Bexhill Central direction sign is a classic SR item, showing the 'Southern Electric' struck through with the electric flash.* **Author**

rigidly from platform roofs near to lamps or on walls. At only 36in long and bearing the station name, these are now highly collectable. This 'hot dog' style of design was first shown at a Railway Executive press conference in February 1948, being referred to as the British Railways Totem. The logo epitomised British Railways to the travelling public – much more easily recognisable than the 'lion and wheel' variants used on locomotive tenders and rolling stock.

Of the six totem variants illustrated (see page 74), Design A was used for main station signs and non-outlined versions used on fascia boards. The other examples were used variously on paperwork, road vehicles, etc.

Totem station signs started in use around

**Above:** *An Isle of Wight (and West Sussex) corner in a collection of Southern enamel. It comprises a selection of running-in boards, totems, targets and stop-boards from different eras. Note the subtle differences in the three fascia poster board headers, bottom right.*
**Author**

1950, and stations were gradually re-signed over a 20-year period. Some stations, receiving totems in the late 1960s, post-dated the 1965 British Rail corporate identity programme which set the ball rolling for the end of providing signage in the regional colours.

Originally, totem station signs had a simple right-angled lip top and bottom, with three bolt-holes drilled therein. With the passage of time, these signs became corroded at the edges and vandals could easily bend the wings at right angles to make the name unreadable. Totems were therefore made more rigid by keeping the top and bottom flange and adding a lip around the edge. With around 20 years of totem manufacturing and by different manufacturers, slight variants are bound to exist – the most obvious being that earlier Southern Region totems were dark green while the later examples (probably from a different manufacturer) were of a lighter green. Some early Eastern Region totems had thicker white lines at the top and bottom.

The Western Region experimented with black and white totems at Bourne End, Devonport, Hayes & Harlington and Langley (Bucks) but, thankfully, the idea did not catch on! Bristol Temple Meads and Birmingham Snow Hill, meanwhile, had a round sign design that incorporated a totem within, in addition to the provision of standard totems.

COULSDON NO...
HORSHAM
CRAWLEY
HOUGHTON BRIDGE POST OFFICE ←— ‹‹
STEYNING
HORSTED KEYNE
HEATHFIELD
ARDINGLY
PLEASE SHOW TICKETS
CHRIST'S HOSPITAL
BRAMLEY & WONERSH

The Midland Region had some 4ft long totems made, such as at Broad Street, and also printed totems on large posters.

Unfortunately, despite all attempts, there was no such thing as ultimate standardisation for BR. The re-signing policy seemed to be left to local divisional management within the regions and this meant that some stations received platform signs/directional signs and/or running-in boards in enamel, but did not receive totems. Some lines had stations that received totems while their neighbouring stations seemed oblivious to modernisation and continued to sport earlier examples of signage such as Southern Railway targets or LMS Hawkseyes right up until British Rail corporate identity replacements arrived. This has resulted in some Southern targets being in very poor condition, rusted and bleached by the sun from around 40 years of exposure!

Some rural lines that were closed in the 1950s only received an enamel running-in board and no totems – they had obviously been candidates for closure many years previously, and did not need unwarranted expenditure!

The corporate identity programme rolled on and many station enamels on the Eastern and London Midland regions lost out to the onslaught of fluorescent lighting with the station name printed on the perspex shade. The Helvetica lettering, black on a white background, brought the first widespread use of lower case lettering in the 1960s, mirroring the European standard that other large bodies were using, such as the National Health Service. It is significant that capital lettered signs started to disappear from our road network at around the same time.

Enamel continued to be the preferred medium for London street signs and Underground signs, but we have seen the last of interesting signage to divert our attentions on the privatised railways today. The branding now owes itself to a cheap strip of coloured vinyl!

There is much interest in collecting enamel signs, mainly from the BR and Grouping eras, and specialist publications and auctions cater for collectors' needs.

### An Idea of Prices (Mid-2001)

Station totem nameboards remain the most popular category of sought-after enamel signs, due to the British Railways era still being within living memory and the youth of most active collectors. As with estate agents, location is everything, followed by rarity and condition. If it is a good name, yet with few known survivors and the enamel is mottled or has lost its shine due to weathering, it will still command a good price.

Examples from closed stations across all regions will always attract keen attention from collectors of the relevant area. Other sought-after locations include the Scottish Highlands with their scenic routes across Rannoch Moor and out onto the West Coast, together with the much lamented Waverley Route. Southern Region totems, away from the close-together stations of suburbia, become of interest when examples are offered from lines where the Southern penetrated Western territory, such as the 'Withered Arm' routes and out to the Atlantic Coast, together with the legendary Somerset & Dorset route and the Isle of Wight.

The North Eastern Region, short-lived and the smallest geographical area, is always of interest, with its signs of a deep tangerine

colour. Many stations were changed out of all recognition with the advent of the Tyne & Wear Metro. With the Eastern Region, closed Lincolnshire and Norfolk locations command a good price, especially holiday towns, which are of interest across the regions. With Midland (apart from closed and Settle & Carlisle stations) and Western Region totems, location and rarity are everything.

Collectors are a funny lot. They all have different reasons for collecting that are many and varied. Examples from railway towns such as Eastleigh and Swindon fetch a good price, while there are those who collect on typographical merit – for example, a long name is used in the rarer Condensed form of Gill Sans to fit the standard width sign, or there is smaller wording also used in the lower panel, or the same station had two different examples extant, some with the word 'AND' and some with an ampersand!

With regard to prices, the minimum £100–£200 slot goes to the sort of South London and North West Kent suburban locations with such salubrious names as Tulse Hill and Herne Hill, with examples surviving in droves, most having gone through Collectors' Corner, Euston, in the 1970s.

The average priced totem for the rest of the country remains in the £300–£500 bracket, with prices rising to nudge four figures for very good locations. Outstanding and sought-after locations at auction would only start bidding at £1,000 to save time.

At the time of writing, recent Western Region signs were realising the following prices: Severn Tunnel Junction – £1,950; Birmingham Snow Hill – £1,050;

**Next pages:** *The following diagrams are from the official BR design register of enamel signs. They show sizes as well as lettering and general style and give an idea of what signs are now most readily to be found; those shown were nearly universal at all but the smallest stations. All the signs would have been available in individual regional colours, as specified to the manufacturers.* ***Author's Collection***

# VARIATIONS OF BRITISH RAILWAYS TOTEM DESIGN

**Design "A"**
Solid with outline.
Coloured.

**Design "B"**
Reverse of "A"

**Design "C"**
Version "B" simplified,
i.e. without outline.

**Design "D"**
Outline Totem with
lettering in self-colour.

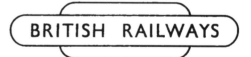

**Design "E"**
Reverse of "D"

**Design "F"**
as "D" with top and
bottom panels hatched.

Wolverhampton Low Level – £1,250; Instow £1,250; Midland Region: Burton on Trent – £2,200; Althorp Park – £2,100, Dent – £1,650; Scottish Region: Joppa – £1,650; Glenfinnan – £2,000; Grantown-on-Spey West – £2,200; North Eastern Region: Burton Salmon – £2,100; Eastern Region: Gedling – £1,300; Southern Region: Budleigh Salterton – £1,650.

At the beginning of 2000, the Totem superleague of all prices over £2,500 belonged to: Stalbridge, Shap, Rugby Central and Instow at £2,600, Waterloo at £2,650, Langley (Bucks) and King's Cross at £2,900, Derby Friargate at £3,000, King's Cross (York Road) at £3,300, Bude at £3,400, Fort William and Stalbridge (again!) at £4,500 and the top slot goes to York at £6,300.

The forerunner of the totem signs on the Southern, the Southern Railway enamel 'target' signs, follow the same basic rules as the totems with regard to location but many examples can vary in condition because of their age. Top target prices of the past have included Corfe Castle at £1,650 and Ryde St Johns at £720.

With the rest of enamel signs, the condition and wording will play a large part in determining the price. Every fair size station had signs hanging from the canopies and smaller enamel doorplates, together with the larger 'running-in' boards to be found near the ends of the platforms. Prices can start at £30–£50 and rise well into three figures for unusual wording. With doorplates, North Eastern tangerine and Scottish light blue examples with wording such as 'Left Luggage', 'Telegrams' etc are going to be more sought after than the common 'Private' and 'Gentlemen' signs. Double-liners such as 'Station Master' are prized across all regions. As to running-in boards, there is a philosophy that 'the more enamel, the smaller the cost' largely due to the problems of transporting or displaying such large signs, but a running-in board for Newton Abbot recently made over £500 – location again!

SMALL NAME SIGNS (LAMP TABLETS)

**DARLINGTON**

Length of Sign 36"    Height of Letters 3"

**ENQUIRIES**

Length of Sign 18"    Depth of Sign 3½"
Height of Letters 1¼"

**SEASON TICKETS**

Length of Sign 18"    Depth of Sign 6"
Height of Letters 1½"

**LADIES WAITING ROOM**

Length of Sign  24"
Depth   ,,   ,,   18"
Height of Letters 3

**STATION MASTER**

Length of Sign  24"
Depth   ,,   ,,   18"
Height of Letters 3"

**TICKETS**

Length of Sign  24"
Depth   ,,   ,,   18
Height of Letters 3

**REFRESHMENTS**

Length of Sign  36"
Depth   ,,   ,,   18"
Height of Letters 3"

**WAY OUT**

Length of Sign   36"
Depth   ,,   ,,   12"
Height of Letters 3

| | |
|---|---|
| Length of Sign | 24" |
| Depth  ,,   ,, | 18" |
| Height of Letters | $1\frac{3}{4}$" |
| ,,   ,, Figure | 10" |

| | |
|---|---|
| Length of Sign | 24" |
| Depth  ,,   ,, | 18" |
| Height of Letters | $1\frac{3}{4}$" |
| ,,   ,, Figure | 9" |
| Length of Arrow | 15" |

| | |
|---|---|
| Length of Sign | 36" |
| Depth  ,,   ,, | 18" |
| Height of Letters | $1\frac{3}{4}$" |

| | |
|---|---|
| Length of Sign | 36" |
| Depth  ,,   ,, | 18" |
| Height of Letters | $1\frac{3}{4}$" |

# CHAPTER 5

# RAILWAY CATERING

## by Tim Petchey

The mention of 'railway catering' immediately transports many people back to the last time they queued for a packet of indifferent crisps and a plastic cup of coffee, with a plastic lid which leaked and scalded their hand. Things have come a long way since the great I. K. Brunel complained of the coffee at the Swindon Refreshment Rooms being brewed from 'bad roast corn' in the 1840s!

It is an established fact that if you sit anyone – particularly a family – on a train to commence a long journey, the first thing they will want to do is eat. The fledgling railway companies were not slow to work this out, so the dining car was born. On-train catering reached its peak in the first dozen or so years of the 20th century, the first class diners at least enjoying sumptuous surroundings and service to match any hotel. Some lines segregated the lesser classes to second and third class dining cars, while a few suffered them in with the 'firsts' just while they dined. The crack expresses of the 1930s carried on the tradition of the prewar days, with the standards on the 'Cornish Riviera', 'Royal Scot', 'Flying Scotsman' and the others second to none.

Work in the kitchen cars almost took on the status of a fine art, with all food preparation carried out on the move. Huge quantities of vegetables boiled in the curious,

tall, narrow pans developed out of necessity so that as many as possible could be fitted on to the restricted area of gas rings. Joints of meat were taken out of the ovens, basted, put back in and eventually carved without spilling the hot fat as the train careered over Crewe South Junction at 70mph. Comradeship among the kitchen staff was an absolute must; imagine working for eight hours in those cramped, chaotic conditions with somebody you particularly disliked!

Buffet cars developed as the demand grew for less formal eating. The great advantage to the railway companies was that the customer would come and fetch the food and take it back to his or her seat to eat it. A few seats were usually available in the buffet but these always seemed to be permanently occupied by people who did not eat anything.

Busier trains, particularly in the days of World War 2, were served by refreshment trolleys – long, narrow affairs which would be propelled along the train, usually by a lady of great skill and determination. At one end was a large urn of boiling water, while the rest of the trolley carried a selection of whatever food was currently available. Cups and plates were transported on the lower shelf.

Cross-country services in the early part of the century were not generally equipped with any form of catering. A peckish

**Above:** *A tall copper saucepan marked 'GWR Hotels'. These were in general hotel and kitchen car use, the narrowness allowing for stoves to be as compact as possible — an important point in an on-board kitchen.* **Author/Winchcombe Railway Museum Collection.**

passenger could, however, order a luncheon basket, which would be prepared at one of the larger stations blessed with refreshment rooms. The wicker basket would contain a plate, knife and fork, and perhaps some cold meat, bread and butter, some fruit and even a small bottle of wine and a glass. The basket lid would invariably be adorned with a small enamel plate stating the place of origin, to which the empty basket should be returned by the train's staff. The North Eastern Railway offered a lighter alternative, packed in a non-returnable cardboard box.

As with all forms of railway catering, the tableware would always be decorated with the name or initials of the owning company. In the few instances of jointly owned rolling stock operating over the lines of two or more companies, this was usually reflected in the markings on the cutlery and china. Hence the knives and forks on the pre-1923 Euston-Glasgow services would be marked 'West Coast Dining Saloons' and the eastern opposition between Kings Cross and Edinburgh 'E.C.J.S.', or East Coast Joint Stock.

In the heyday of day excursions to the races or to the seaside, the excursion carriages would usually be emptied of their passengers and then taken to a convenient location to be cleaned out and serviced, ready for the return trip. Among other duties this entailed washing up all the tableware used on the outward journey. Human nature being what it is, with slightly chipped china or heavily soiled items, it was easier to heave them out with the waste food than to return them for replacement or whatever. Human nature being what it is again, the local railwaymen of the district would rummage through the pile, to see what was worth taking home. This phenomenon has resulted in a great deal of material surviving, to be treasured by today's collector.

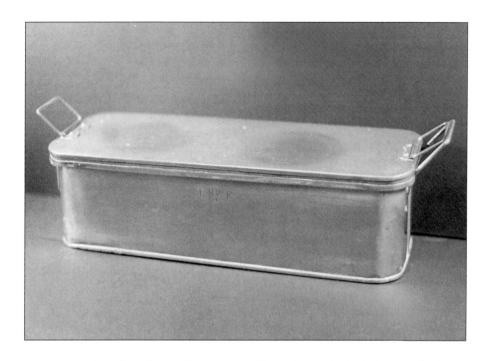

A great variety of catering establishments have been developed over the years at stations. Larger stations would have several refreshment rooms accessible from all parts of the station, while some smaller termini or junction stations might have just one room, with the trade supplemented by opening as well to the non-travelling public. In some villages this doubled as the local café and pub. Often such facilities were not operated directly by the railway but let out on a franchise to a tenant, who would try many ways to increase his or her overall trade.

Indeed, a few companies decided not to concern themselves with catering to the masses at all, and let the whole operation to a firm of contractors. The best known of these operators was probably Messrs Spiers & Pond, at various times contractors to the London & South Western and later to the Southern, as well as other lines.

Busy junction stations, where passengers might have only a few minutes before continuing their journeys, or indeed might not need to leave their train at all, would sometimes feature a trolley service on the appropriate platform. This vehicle would be larger than its on-train cousin but would carry a similar hot water urn and selection of food.

Sometimes the cutlery and other tableware used in a particular refreshment room or station would carry not only the railway company's name but the name of the location as well. These items have lately become highly prized by the collector.

The other land-bound home of public railway catering was of course the railway hotel. These were usually among the most grand of their breed, benefiting from the huge financial and physical infrastructure provided by their owning railway companies. The sites for these hotels were chosen for their proximity to centres of trade and

**Above:** *This rather tired-looking item is in fact a roly-poly pudding tin of LMS vintage, made at Wolverton Carriage Works specifically for the dining service. Few such items have survived, partly because people have not always appreciated their historic significance.* **Author/Winchcombe Railway Museum Collection.**

**Right:** *For staff rather than public catering use, this 8-pint cast-iron kettle was made for the LMS.* **Author/Winchcombe Railway Museum Collection.**

**Above:** *A wicker luncheon basket, provided to passengers by the LNWR's Lancaster refreshment rooms. The enamel label helped to ensure that most of these were returned to base after use, which was quite a logistical exercise in itself!*
**Author/Winchcombe Railway Museum Collection**

commerce, areas of scenic beauty, or sporting greatness, but always with easy access to the railway station. Hotels, and to a lesser extent other outlets, purveyed specially packaged products such as beer, wines, spirits and biscuits, a kind of forerunner to today's 'own brand' goods.

Neither does the story stop with public establishments. Railways were obviously huge employers with many mouths to feed. Many such 'company's servants' would make their own arrangements for meals, taking their sandwiches and bottle of cold tea to work with them. Others would have rudimentary arrangements to make a brew as and when necessary. Larger establishments might be provided with a staff canteen, a sort of scaled-down refreshment room operation. The writer well remembers attending some sort of meeting in such a canteen at London, Victoria station and rummaging through the

cutlery boxes to find the pieces marked with the initials of the London, Chatham & Dover Railway.

A step up from the staff canteen is the Staff Association. Here the railway worker could spend some leisure time, perhaps in the library or bar, or partaking of a reasonable meal at a reasonable price. Tokens could be purchased in advance and exchanged for meals when required. Often these places would have their own marked tableware, in part to discourage pilfering of the precious resources.

At a few locations the railway employee who desired something better than canteen fare could join a Dining Club. These were usually 'mutual societies' which operated on a non-profit-making basis, with the support of the host railway company in providing decent and pleasant surroundings for meals.

During the two World Wars, each of which saw huge numbers of service personnel travelling alone or in small groups on the country's railways, special canteens were set up to provide them with 'char and a wad'. Normally run by volunteers, these canteens were often equipped with their own distinctive mugs and spoons, and whatever other tableware they might require. Surviving items from these ephemeral institutions are especially rare.

**Above:** *An even rarer survivor is this cardboard 'Light Luncheon' box, once provided to a passenger on the North Eastern Railway and carrying an advert for the company's hotels. By what lucky chance, we must wonder, did this box avoid almost immediate destruction, let alone last down to the present day?* **Author/Winchcombe Railway Museum Collection.**

No account of railway catering operations would be complete without mention of the considerable fleet of railway-owned ships. Here one could find levels of service to match that of the best hotel, as well as that of the lowliest buffet! The ships were provided with substantial stocks of silverware and china, and were the equal of vessels owned by the big shipping lines.

**Above:** *The uncompromising china mark on GWR on-train services crockery, presumably an item from a buffet or trolley rather than the stylish environments of a 'Cornish Riviera' restaurant car, whose patrons probably expected something a little less abrupt* **Author/Winchcombe Railway Museum Collection**

**Above:** *The GWR Hotels were equally blunt in ensuring the best chance for their catering wares to return to base, should a passenger take them onto a train. This is a post-1935 example.* **Author/Winchcombe Railway Museum Collection**

In the 1970s, when the old Midland Grand Hotel at St Pancras station was the headquarters of the then British Transport Hotels, the writer was able to make an amazing trip of discovery into this building. An appointment was made and the date duly arrived. After checking in with the security man by the main entrance, I was directed to the appropriate office and made contact with a gentleman from the Stores Department. He took me down into the bowels of the earth below that magnificent pile, through the then still operating laundry, into a vaulted cellar. Then he paused to unlock a large, creaking door, disappeared inside and turned on the light. Before me was the nearest thing I shall ever see to Aladdin's Cave. All around the walls and across the centre of the room were racks of shelving, each groaning under the weight of piles of silverware. There, as well as all the usual knives, forks and spoons, were grape scissors, nutcrackers, swizzle sticks, toastracks and bread baskets. There were tureen covers as big as dustbin lids, champagne buckets, sundae dishes, coffee pots. All of these items had been withdrawn from service and were available for sale. Between them they represented most of the main line railway companies of the 20th century and a good many others as well. I well remember one item marked 'Cook's Nile Service' – never quite sure how that one got there!

The arrangement was that you could select whichever items you wanted and they would be put on one side. You then left and went home to await a letter which would list the individual price for each item, based on

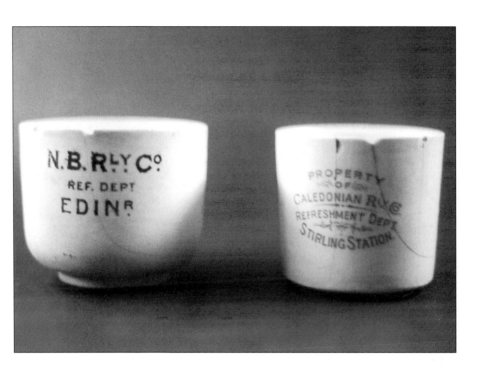

**Above:** *Despite their rather used state, these pre-Grouping teacups remain highly collectable. That on the left is from the North British Railway's refreshment department at Edinburgh, the other has been clearly marked by the Caledonian as belonging at Stirling.* **Author/Winchcombe Railway Museum Collection.**

**Right:** *The LMS Hotels china mark seems a little less forbidding to users. Some of the company's hotels had their individual marks instead of this corporate one.* **Author/Winchcombe Railway Museum Collection.**

the price BTH would have to pay for a similar new item. If you still wished to proceed with the purchase of any or all of the items, you sent in a cheque and awaited a letter saying that your items were ready for collection. The whole process took about two weeks. Subsequent visits revealed dwindling stock levels until eventually the hoard had been dispersed. Ah! What memories!

*Many of the items illustrated in this chapter, and many other items, can be seen on display as part of the collections of Winchcombe Railway Museum.*

**Below:** *Glasgow & South Western Hotels, while keeping to a corporate image, managed something a little more stylish in design than some of their neighbours. Rarity value from this relatively small concern now adds to this piece's value.*
**Author/Winchcombe Railway Museum Collection**

**Above:** *The LMS-owned Gleneagles Hotel is one example of an establishment with sufficient prestige to have its own china mark.*
**Author/Winchcombe Railway Museum Collection**

**Above:** *The South Eastern Railway managed to bring some thought to the design of the Deal Hotel china mark.* **Author/Winchcombe Railway Museum Collection**

**Above:** *A fish fork from Great Eastern Railway restaurant car stocks. The marking is blunt and uncompromising.* **Author/Winchcombe Railway Museum Collection.**

**Above:** *East Coast Joint Stock cutlery had a rather grander marking. This service, operated by the Great Northern, North Eastern and North British Railways between Kings Cross and Edinburgh Waverley, marked its cutlery at the hand-end — altogether more dignified!* **Author/Winchcombe Railway Museum Collection.**

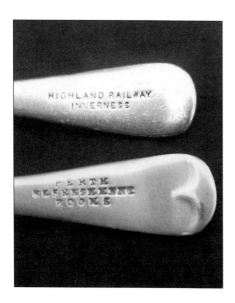

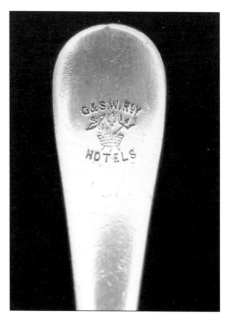

**Above:** *Cutlery marks of the Highland and Caledonian Railways, both specific to one location.* **Author/Winchcombe Railway Museum Collection.**

**Above:** *The Glasgow & South Western Hotels cutlery mark matched its china mark.* **Author/Winchcombe Railway Museum Collection.**

**Left:** *A London & North Eastern half-pint beer bottle in green glass, with embossed lettering.*
**Author/Winchcombe Railway Museum Collection**

**Below:** *An idea of the range of tableware the railways provided, which gives an insight into the expectations of the patrons: from the left, a swizzle stick (cocktail mixer), lobster pick, nutcrackers and grape scissors. All are from the LNER.*
**Author/Winchcombe Railway Museum Collection**

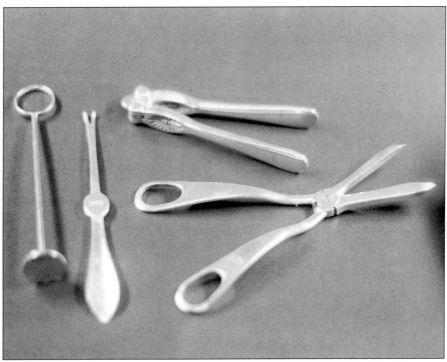

**Above:** *Workers' ware can be as interesting as that for passengers. Left, an example of early plastic, a staff beaker from the LMS canteens and hostels service; right, an enamel pint mug for canteen use, with a stylish 'GWR' monogram to discourage wandering stock.* **Author/Winchcombe Railway Museum Collection.**

**Above:** *Six canteen tokens from Derby Works, LMS. Staff would purchase these in advance to pay for meals, each day having its own colour and shape.* **Author/Winchcombe Railway Museum Collection.**

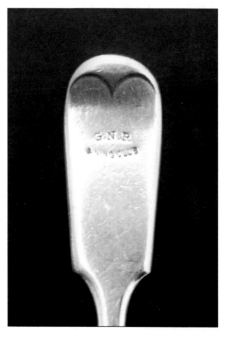

**Above:** *Cutlery mark of the GNR Dining Club. One wonders now whether these were more or less likely to be 'lost' than stock from public services.* **Author/Winchcombe Railway Museum Collection.**

**Above:** *This mug must have an interesting history, apart from being a real rarity now. It is china and was provided for the Sailors & Soldiers Canteen at Crewe station during World War 1.* **Author/ Winchcombe Railway Museum Collection**

**Above:** *The Southern Railway was very proud of its steamer services, whether the short- or longer-haul Channel crossings, or the humble ferry to the Isle of Wight. This is the china mark used in its vessels' catering rooms.* **Author/Winchcombe Railway Museum Collection**

**Above:** *A china cream tot jug from the SR Shipping Services and a GWR Hotels milk jug show how restrained decoration was employed to good effect on railway crockery in the Grouping years.* **Author/Winchcombe Railway Museum Collection.**

# CHAPTER 6

# RAILWAY PAPERWORK

## by Tim Petchey

Ever since there have been railways, they have generated paperwork. At the dawn of the 19th century, when simple tramroads carried horse-drawn wagons of stone or coal, each load had its weigh-ticket, each carter his time sheet. Plans and drawings had to be produced to guide the builders of these routes, contracts for their construction had to be let, shareholders found and shares issued.

All public lines had to have the approval of Parliament before construction could begin. This gave rise to prospectuses, letters of support (and of objection), petitions and finally, hopefully, the Act of Parliament which authorised construction. With a good many of the very early railway companies of the 1830s and 1840s, the only surviving artefacts which today's collector can hope to acquire are documents such as receipts for sums paid for shares, interest warrants and general letters, often with quite elaborate printed headings.

From the same period, indeed up until the beginning of the 20th century, property owners were approached in order to obtain the necessary land to build the lines. As with all sales of land, conveyances and all manner of wayleaves and assent forms were required to keep the solicitors busy, and it is these same solicitors who diligently squirreled away these documents in their store rooms. As the provincial law firms began to

modernise, perhaps with new blood in the partnerships, so some of the musty old documents were turned out, to be fallen upon eagerly by the late 20th century collector.

Although the traditional Edmondson card railway ticket falls outside the description of 'paperwork', the early examples of passenger ticket followed the pattern of those used on the old stage and mail coaches. They were each written out by hand on a sheet of paper, then cut or torn off individually.

By the 1870s the country's railway system was nearing its greatest and busiest. The amount of paperwork then in daily use was phenomenal. Every parcel had to have a consignment note filled in and signed by the sender; the relevant details were then entered on a waybill, which accompanied the parcel to its destination station. On arrival the parcel could require delivery by the road van or alternatively await collection. Trucks of coal had to be invoiced, each truck had a label filled in and attached and consignees had to be notified of the truck's arrival.

Every discrepancy, mislaid umbrella, damaged package or wrongly directed parcel was chased up with a memo to the sending station, sometimes to be returned with that station's comments written at right angles to the original, more often answered with another memo. Where traffic originating on the lines of one railway passed to another

Whitehaven and Furness Junction Railway,

Secretary & General Manager's Office,

M
26/74.

Whitehaven 18 Jan'y 1866.

Dear Sir,

Enclosed, I beg to hand you transfer Certificate of twelve Shares in your name and forward Share Certificates by Book Post.

Please acknowledge receipt.

I am,

Yours truly

1 Encl:

W. Cook
Secretary

James Irving Esq
Carlisle

during its journey, the payment had to be apportioned to each company, according to the distance travelled on each line. This applied equally to passengers as to goods or parcels, and so the Railway Clearing House was set up by the main railway companies in order to facilitate these calculations. Every station on every line then had to submit monthly returns of all kinds of traffic sent and received to and from every other station. The mountains of paperwork at the RCH offices in London must have been a sight to behold!

Many stations were in the habit of keeping the waybills which arrived with traffic, copies of those forwarded, memos, notices from District Goods Managers and anything else, in case there should ever be the need to refer to them. In most cases these were periodically thrown out or burnt, but happily in just a few places the dusty bundles remained undisturbed in the station or goods shed loft for a good deal longer. Probably the two largest of these surviving hoards were at Skipton and Mansfield, both on the Midland Railway. Material of this kind from these two stations can be found in many sales of railway ephemera and indeed in many such collections.

The main channels of communication between stations were the telegraph, the 'Urgent Train Message' and the memorandum. The telegraph system was only of use fairly locally, or within the limits of one particular railway, and in any case its use for non-urgent purposes was frowned upon. The person wishing to send a message would write this down on a 'Telegraphic despatch' form and sign it. It would then be handed to the telegraph operator for transmission, the operator retaining the original for the time being. The operator at the receiving station would write down the message on a similar form to pass to the recipient. Urgent train messages would be used where the telegraph was not available. In this case the originator would write the message on the prescribed form, address it and hand it to the guard of the next train in the right direction. In due course the message would find its way to the required location. Memos were the general, everyday means of communication, and were carried around the country in huge numbers.

An interesting addition to the used waybills and invoices which accompanied the traffic would be the rubber stamp impressions gained along the way. The guard of each train handling these forms was required to sign each one, so that its progress might be checked if a problem should arise. Many guards obtained a rubber stamp of their name and possibly their operating base and railway company, to speed up the process of the paperwork. While those stations handling great amounts of traffic might be provided with waybills carrying a printed station of origin, most such names had to be written or rubber-stamped at the head of each form.

Each station booking office was equipped with a set of books in which to record all types of transaction. Ticket stock levels were entered at the close of business each day, and cloakroom receipts, parcels inward and outward, staff timesheets and pay all duly recorded. Excess fare and excess luggage tickets were issued, along with cloakroom tickets, weighbridge tickets and parcel labels. Passengers' luggage had to be labelled with the name of the destination station, so that the guard would know which station to unload it at. The luggage labels themselves were usually printed with the company name

No. 4

# ELY VALLEY EXTENSION RAILWAYS.

(Incorporation of Company; Railways in Extension of Ely Valley
Railway; Traffic and other arrangements with the Llynvi Valley
Railway, the Ely Valley Railway, the Great Western Railway,
and the South Wales Railway Companies; Power to the Ely
Valley Company to subscribe; Running powers over the Ely
Valley Railway and the Llynvi Valley Railway; Amendment of
Acts.)

*13.* *December*, 1862.

Gentlemen,

I beg to acknowledge the receipt, on or
previously to the 15th of this instant, December, of
your Letter relative to the contemplated application
to Parliament for the above Bill, and request you
will return me as * *assenting* in
respect of such Undertaking.

I am, &c.,

*W. W. Bassett*

*Messrs. Elsdale and Byrne,*
  *R. W. Williams, Esq.*

* Insert "assenting," "dissenting," or "neutral."

94

**MR. BRASSEY'S** *Compliments*

*to* Mr. *Paxton*

*and would be glad to be favored with his company in an*

*excursion over the Buckinghamshire Line of Railway, on*

*Tuesday, the 26th instant.*

*The Train will leave Bletchley, at* 11, A. M.;

*Winslow,* 11, 30; *Buckingham,* 12; *Brackley,* 12, 30;

*arriving at Banbury, at* 1 *o'clock.*

*On its return the Train will leave Banbury, at* 2,

P. M.; *Brackley,* 2, 20; *Buckingham,* 2, 40; *arriving at*

*Winslow, at* 3, P. M.; *where refreshment will be provided.*

BUCKINGHAM, *th*
March *18* 1850.

*An Answer is respectfully*
*solicited, as soon as convenient.*

*S H*

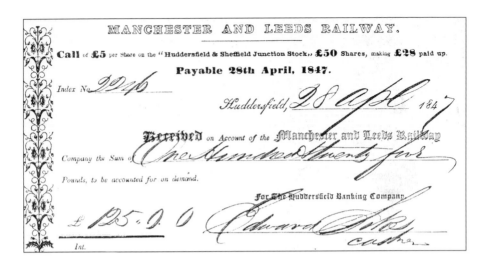

MANCHESTER AND LEEDS RAILWAY.

Call of £5 per Share on the "Huddersfield & Sheffield Junction Stock," £50 Shares, making £28 paid up.

**Payable 28th April, 1847.**

Index No. _____

Huddersfield, 28 Apl 1847

Received on Account of the Manchester and Leeds Railway Company the Sum of _One Hundred Twenty five_

Pounds, to be accounted for on demand.

For the Huddersfield Banking Company.

£ 125.9.0

Int.

and the required station, sometimes giving the route to be travelled. Each station therefore had to carry a stock of all such labels relevant to its traffic.

Instruction booklets covered every part of railway operating and were to be found in each establishment: instructions for signalling trains in fog or falling snow, for loading specific types of traffic to specific destinations, for the prevention of accidents, for the extinction of fire. Notices of temporary speed restrictions or diversions were issued to all train staff; guards' journals detailed the working of every journey. Locomotives developing problems were reported on a casualty form on arrival, crippled wagons likewise.

Every signalbox had a train register book in which the times of the various telegraph and bell code signals for each passing train were entered. On some single line railways a paper ticket was issued to the driver of a train as authority to proceed on the single line, safe in the knowledge that he would not meet a train coming the other way.

**Previous page:** *Invitation from the construction contractor, Mr Brassey, for an excursion over the Buckinghamshire Railway before its public opening.*
**Winchcombe Railway Museum Collection**

**Above:** *Receipt for a further call on the Huddersfield & Sheffield Junction shares. By now the company has been taken over by the Manchester & Leeds Railway. 28 April 1847.*

For the general public, the railways issued timetables which enabled people to plan their journeys, handbills to advise of special excursions or discounted fares, and posters to display the delights of faraway holiday resorts. Savings schemes would enable the holiday expenses to be spread over a longer period, while booklets or leaflets pointed out places of interest on the journey.

Railway paperwork is indeed a huge subject and will provide a fascinating source for a collection, either on its own or in conjunction with other aspects of our railway past.

*All photographs by the author, and documents from the collection of Winchcombe Railway Museum. Some of these and other documents can be seen on display at the Museum.*

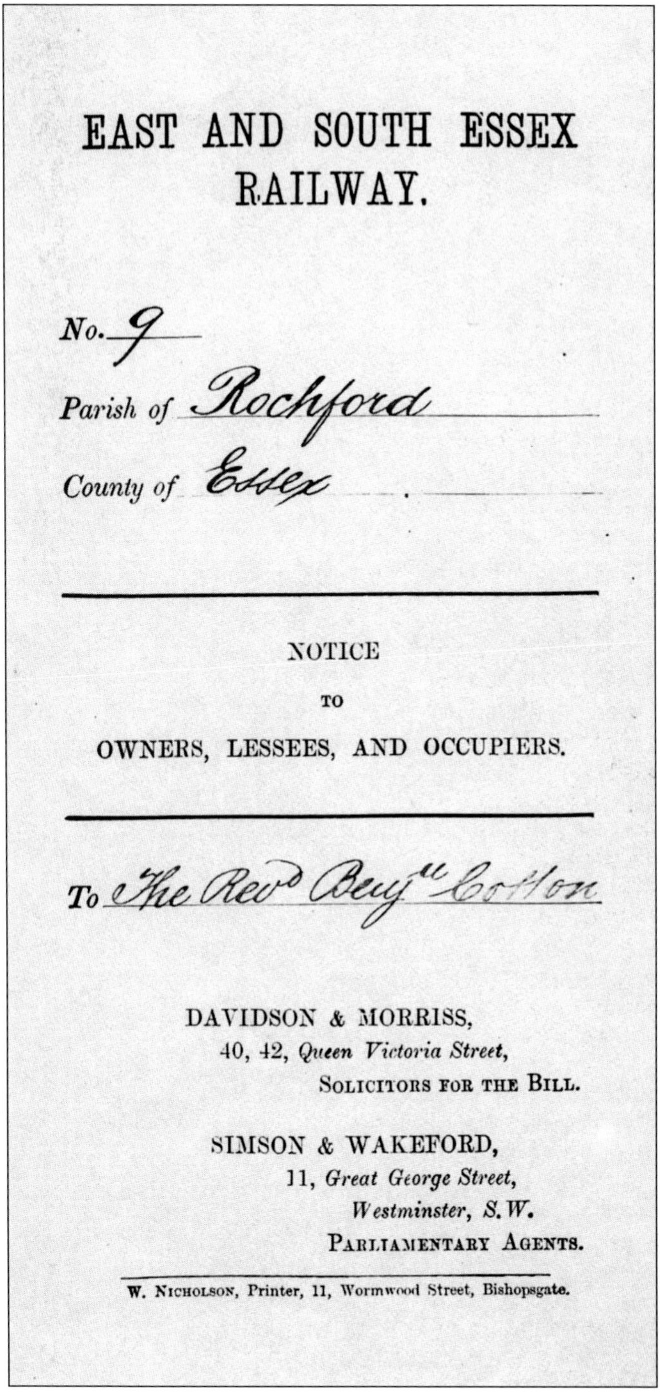

**Right:** *Front page of a 'Notice to owners, Lessees and Occupiers', re acquisition of land for building the East & South Essex Railway, 1881.* **Winchcombe Railway Museum Collection**

# EAST AND SOUTH ESSEX RAILWAY.

No. *9*

Parish of *Rochford*

County of *Essex*

## NOTICE

### TO

## OWNERS, LESSEES, AND OCCUPIERS.

To *The Revd Benjn Cotton*

**DAVIDSON & MORRISS,**
40, 42, *Queen Victoria Street,*
SOLICITORS FOR THE BILL.

**SIMSON & WAKEFORD,**
11, *Great George Street,*
*Westminster, S.W.*
PARLIAMENTARY AGENTS.

W. NICHOLSON, Printer, 11, Wormwood Street, Bishopsgate.

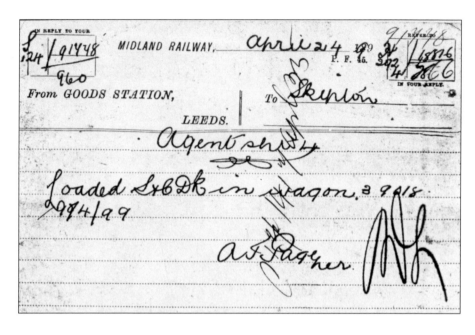

**Above:** *Midland Railway memorandum from Goods station, Leeds, to Skipton, 24 April 1899.*
**Winchcombe Railway Museum Collection**

| | O.S. 15498. |
|---|---|

**U. T. M.** LONDON & NORTH EASTERN RAILWAY **U.T.M.**

Urgent Train Message.     Immediate and Important.

Sent by............Train.    From......................193....

## To the TELEGRAPH OFFICE,
## L. & N. E. Railway,
## .............Station.

For.......................

.............................

**Above:** *LNER Urgent Train Message form, unused.* **Winchcombe Railway Museum Collection**

# GREAT CENTRAL RAILWAY

## CC 2709

Weighing Machine.

_____ 192

Name _____

Species _____

| Charge for Weighing. | d. | Tons | Cwts. | Qrs. |
|---|---|---|---|---|
| Gross ................. | | | | |
| Tare as stated...... | | | | |
| „ as weighed ... | | | | |
| Net............ | | | | |

The Great Central Rly. Co. will not be responsible for the Weights between Buyer and Seller.

# GREAT CENTRAL RAILWAY

## CC 2705

Weighing Machine.

_____ 192

Name _____

Species _____

| Charge for Weighing. | d. | Tons | Cwts. | Qrs. |
|---|---|---|---|---|
| Gross ................. | | | | |
| Tare as stated...... | | | | |
| „ as weighed ... | | | | |
| Net............ | | | | |

The Great Central Rly. Co. will not be responsible for the Weights between Buyer and Seller.

# GREAT CENTRAL RAILWAY

## CC 2710

Weighing Machine.

_____ 192

Name _____

Species _____

| Charge for Weighing, | d. | Tons | Cwts. | Qrs. |
|---|---|---|---|---|
| Gross ................. | | | | |
| Tare as stated...... | | | | |
| „ as weighed ... | | | | |
| Net............ | | | | |

The Great Central Rly. Co. will not be responsible for the Weights between Buyer and Seller.

# GREAT CENTRAL RAILWAY

## CC 2706

Weighing Machine.

_____ 192

Name _____

Species _____

| Charge for Weighing, | d. | Tons | Cwts. | Qrs. |
|---|---|---|---|---|
| Gross ................. | | | | |
| Tare as stated...... | | | | |
| „ as weighed ... | | | | |
| Net............ | | | | |

The Great Central Rly. Co. will not be responsible for the Weights between Buyer and Seller.

**Above:** _Block of four unused weighing machine tickets, Great Central Railway._
**Winchcombe Railway Museum Collection**

**GREAT WESTERN RAILWAY.** (323 P)

**EXCESS LUGGAGE NOTE.**

No. **35**

_____o'clock Train_____day of_____19____

From_____to_____

_____Passengers_____Class.

No. of Packages_____

| | CWTS. | QRS. | LBS. |
|---|---|---|---|
| Gross Weight | | | |
| Weight allowed | | | |
| Weight charged | | | |

@_____per lb.   £   :   :

_____Booking Clerk.

Passengers are requested to see the Company's labels placed upon each article of their Luggage. The Company is not accountable for any package containing articles coming within the Carriers' Act, 1830, above the value of £25, unless entered and paid for accordingly.

NOTE.—This Ticket to be produced on demand and given up when claiming the luggage.

750 pads, 200 lvs. (3 patts). B.M.23/1 1946 (8) S.

**Above:** *Unused GWR excess luggage note, printed in 1946.* **Winchcombe Railway Museum Collection**

**Right:** *Weston, Clevedon & Portishead Railway excess fare receipt from Colehouse Lane to Weston, 9 March 1939.* **Winchcombe Railway Museum Collection**

Weston, Clevedon & Portishead Railway

NOT AVAILABLE

When this Corner is cut off at end of Journey

Excess Fare Receipt No. A **9820**

Issued at...

Date...9/3/39... Train...

Excessed from...Colehouse L

to...Weston...

| | Single | Return | Fare | £ | s | d. |
|---|---|---|---|---|---|---|
| ......Class without Ticket ...... | | | | | | |
| ......Class travelled on | | | | | | |
| No. of Ticket held ..... | | | | | | |
| 3rd Class to 1st ...... | | | | | | |
| ......Class, Children over age .. | | | | | | |
| Dogs accompanied by passenger | | | | | | |
| Bicycles    „    „ | | | | | | |
| Prams ...... | | | | | | |
| Folding Prams ...... | | | | | | |
| TOTAL ... | | | | | | 1/8 |

TO BE GIVEN TO PASSENGERS

Collector...

TO BE SHOWN OR GIVEN UP ON DEMAND

Issued subject to Conditions shown in Public Notices and Time Books. Available on day of issue and train stated only.

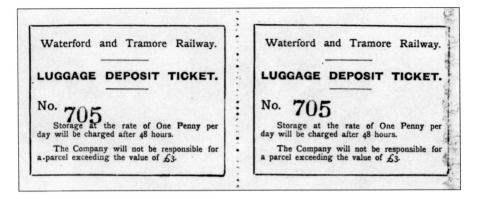

| Waterford and Tramore Railway. | Waterford and Tramore Railway. |
|---|---|
| **LUGGAGE DEPOSIT TICKET.** | **LUGGAGE DEPOSIT TICKET.** |
| No. **705** | No. **705** |
| Storage at the rate of One Penny per day will be charged after 48 hours. | Storage at the rate of One Penny per day will be charged after 48 hours. |
| The Company will not be responsible for a parcel exceeding the value of £3. | The Company will not be responsible for a parcel exceeding the value of £3. |

[1916 O.]

**London Brighton & South Coast Railway.**

Tolls Paid at Hayling Bridge_____ 189

| No. **37125** | D. | AMOUNT. |
|---|---|---|
| Foot Passenger .........@ 0½ | | |
| Horse, Mule, or Ass ... „ 1½ | | |
| Ditto, Carrying Double „ 2 | | |
| Beast, Sheep, Calf, Pig „ 0½ | | |
| Ditto, per Score .........„ 7 | | |
| Carriage_____horse | | |
| Wagon or Dray____horse | | |
| Cart_____horse | | |
| Hearse_____horse | | |

**HUNDRED OF MANHOOD AND SELSEY TRAMWAYS, Co., Ltd.**

**CLOAK ROOM.**

This deposit is accepted by the Company subject to the conditions endorsed on the back of this Ticket.

Date _____ 26/8/25

No. 77 ____ 4

ARTICLES.

Excess _____ Days _____

Declared Value £ _____

Company not liable for Articles beyond £10 in value unless extra value be declared.

---

G.N.R.B. OMNIBUS SERVICES — G.N. 4446 / Sheet I

**Parcels Record, Receipt and Ticket Book** — E 8261

Description of Packages_____ Wt_____lbs.

From_____ (Sender)

_____ (Address)

To_____ (Consignee)

_____ (Full Address)

Received in Good Order by_____ 25/9 19 58

---

GN 4412/5

**G.N.R. CLOAK ROOM**

_____ STATION

No. **D 23509**

Date Deposit_____ Date of Delivery_____

Name of Depositor_____

| No. | DESCRIPTION of ARTICLES |
|---|---|
| 9 | |

| Amount Paid | Storage Charge |
|---|---|
| **8d** | s. d. |

The above charge covers the day of deposit and the following day, after which excess charges will be made

FOR CONDITIONS SEE BACK

**Above:** *(i) Luggage deposit ticket with counterfoil, Waterford & Tramore Railway. (ii) London, Brighton & South Coast Railway toll ticket for Hayling Bridge, 28 August 1898. (iii) Cloakroom ticket, Hundred of Manhood & Selsey Tramways Co, 26 May 1925. (iv) GNR (I) Board Omnibus Services parcels ticket, 20 September 1958. (v) GNR (Ireland) cloakroom ticket.* **Winchcombe Railway Museum Collection**

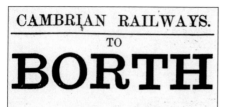

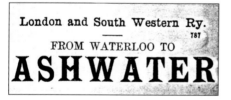

**Above:** *Selection of luggage labels, simple paper designs to be pasted on to passengers' luggage to indicate the destination station.* **Winchcombe Railway Museum Collection**

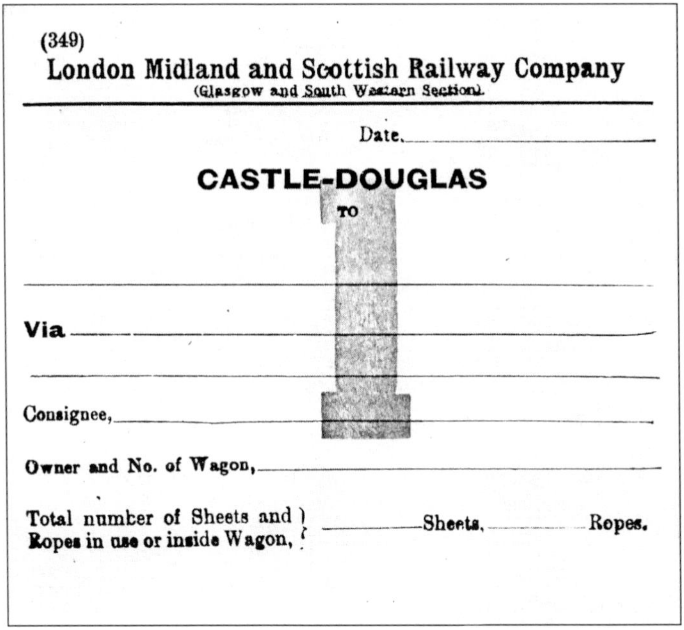

(349)

# London Midland and Scottish Railway Company
### (Glasgow and South Western Section)

Date.

## CASTLE-DOUGLAS
### TO

Via

Consignee,

Owner and No. of Wagon,

Total number of Sheets and }
Ropes in use or inside Wagon, } _____ Sheets, _____ Ropes.

**Left:** *Unused wagon label from the early days of the LMS. The label follows the pattern of the former Glasgow & South Western Railway.* **Winchcombe Railway Museum Collection**

**Below:** *Unused train staff ticket, Schull to Ballydehob, on the Schull & Skibbereen Tramway & Light Railway.* **Winchcombe Railway Museum Collection**

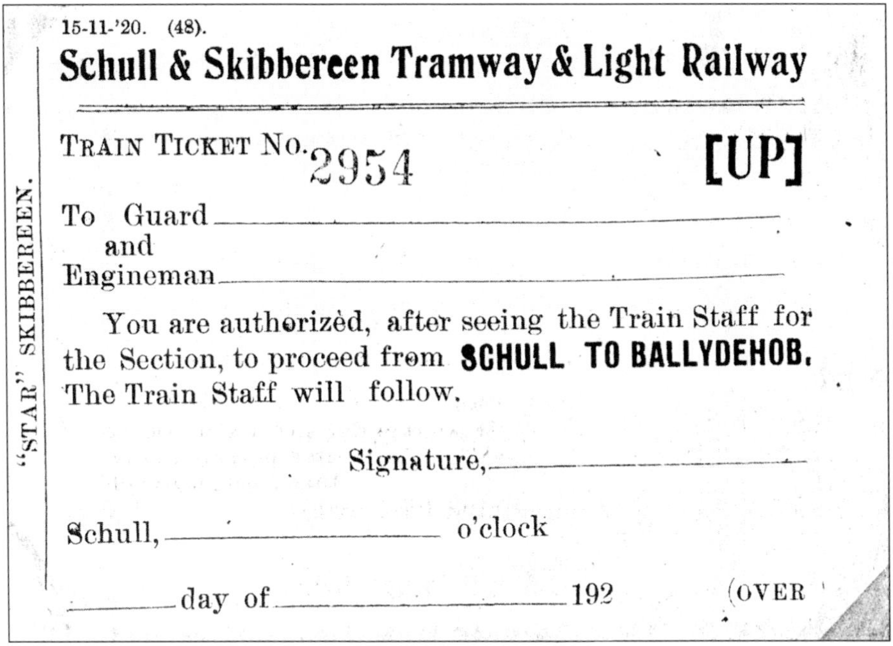

15-11-'20. (48).

# Schull & Skibbereen Tramway & Light Railway

TRAIN TICKET No. 2954                    **[UP]**

To Guard
and
Engineman

You are authorized, after seeing the Train Staff for the Section, to proceed from **SCHULL TO BALLYDEHOB.** The Train Staff will follow.

Signature,

Schull, _____ o'clock

_____ day of _____ 192        (OVER

"STAR" SKIBBEREEN.

**ERO. 20397**

**L.M.&S.R.**    No 3608

# DOWN TRAIN STAFF TICKET
## STONEHOUSE & NAILSWORTH BRANCH.

TRAIN No.

TO THE DRIVER,
You are authorised, after seeing the Train Staff for the Section, to proceed from **STONEHOUSE STATION TO DUDBRIDGE SIDINGS**, and the Train Staff will follow.

DATE

Signature of Person in Charge

This Ticket must be given up by the Driver, immediately on arrival, to the person in charge of the Staff Working at the place to which he is authorised to proceed, to be cancelled and forwarded to the Chief Operating Manager.

**ERO. 20394**
**O.P.2**

**L.M.&S.R.**    No. 1999

# DOWN TRAIN STAFF TICKET
## HAWES BRANCH.

TRAIN No.

TO THE DRIVER,
You are authorised, after seeing the Train Staff for the Section, to proceed from **GARSDALE JUNCTION to HAWES STATION**, and the Train Staff will follow.

DATE

Signature of Person in Charge

This Ticket must be given up by the Driver, immediately on arrival, to the person in charge of the Staff Working at the place to which he is authorised to proceed, to be cancelled and forwarded to the Chief Operating Manager.

**Above:** *LMS train staff tickets, each specifying the particular section of single line railway to which they apply.* **Winchcombe Railway Museum Collection**

**Right:** *GWR handbill for the withdrawal of passenger services on the former Cleobury Mortimer & Ditton Priors Light Railway, July 1938.* **Winchcombe Railway Museum Collection**

# SPECIAL NOTICE

## DISCONTINUANCE OF
## PASSENGER TRAIN SERVICE

BETWEEN

# CLEOBURY MORTIMER

AND

# DITTON PRIORS

The Great Western Railway give notice that on and from MONDAY, SEPTEMBER 26th, 1938, the Passenger Train service on the above Line will be withdrawn and the following trains cancelled :—

> 9.30 a.m. Cleobury Mortimer to Ditton Priors.
> 2.24 p.m. (Wednesdays only) Cleobury Mortimer to Ditton Priors.
> 5.20 p.m. Cleobury Mortimer to Ditton Priors.
> 11.10 a.m. Ditton Priors to Cleobury Mortimer.
> 3.50 p.m. (Wednesdays only) Ditton Priors to Cleobury Mortimer.
> 6.23 p.m. Ditton Priors to Cleobury Mortimer.

The Platforms at the undermentioned places will be closed to Passengers :—

| | |
|---|---|
| CLEOBURY TOWN HALT | ASTON BOTTERELL SIDING |
| DETTON FORD SIDING | BURWARTON HALT |
| PRESCOTT SIDING | CLEOBURY NORTH CROSSING |
| STOTTESDON HALT | DITTON PRIORS HALT |

The Company will continue to run one Goods train in each direction over the Line on week-days only, and so afford facilities for the conveyance of Parcels traffic, Minerals, Livestock and General Merchandise to and from the above-mentioned places.

Particulars of the arrangements may be obtained on application to the Station Master, Cleobury Mortimer, Mr. J. E. POTTER, Divisional Superintendent, Worcester (Shrub Hill Station) (Telephone 1530), or Mr. J. A. WARREN-KING, District Goods Manager, Worcester (Shrub Hill Station) (Telephone 1530).

PADDINGTON STATION,
July, 1938.

JAMES MILNE,
General Manager.

8,40). Printed in Great Britain by WYMAN & SONS LTD., London, Reading and Fakenham.—519.

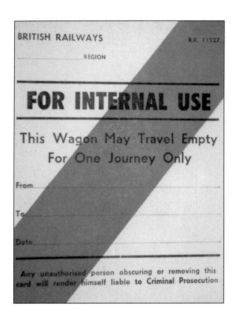

**Above:** *Unused BR wagon label for use on a condemned wagon, which might make only one last journey before scrapping.*
**Winchcombe Railway Museum Collection**

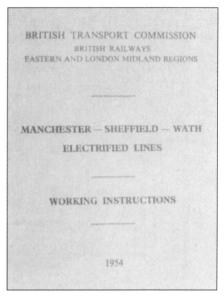

**Above:** *Working instructions booklet for the Manchester-Sheffield-Wath electrified lines of BR Eastern and LM Regions, 1954.*
**Winchcombe Railway Museum Collection**

**Above:** *Timetable book of LMS passenger services, 16 June to 5 October 1947.*
**Winchcombe Railway Museum Collection**

**Above:** *Timetable booklet of the GNR (Ireland), 15 June 1952.*
**Winchcombe Railway Museum Collection**

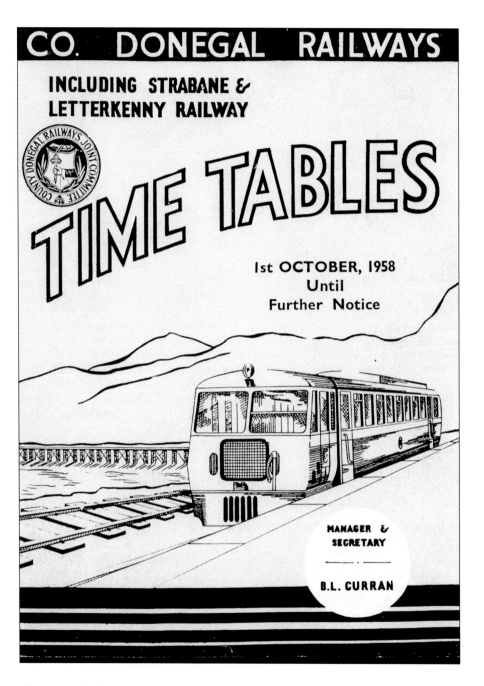

**Above:** *Timetable booklet of the County Donegal Railways Joint Committee, 1 October 1958.*
**Winchcombe Railway Museum Collection**

## CHAPTER 7

# TICKETS (AND ASSOCIATED ITEMS)

## by Michael Farr

Tickets are probably the most convenient and compact type of railwayana to collect – until one expands to include associated ticket equipment such as issuing and cancelling machines or, as in my case, ticket printing machines weighing over a ton!

Today, tickets on most British railway companies are simply checked on trains and do not have to be given up at the end of a journey, so a personal collection can easily be started straight away. Yesterday's collectors were not so fortunate and a stern uniformed official invariably greeted them at the end of their journey, hand outstretched to accept the ticket meekly proffered. Thus older railway tickets are generally in short supply, whereas bus and tram enthusiasts could not only keep their own tickets but even ask the conductor whether they could empty the used ticket box on the vehicle.

Tickets have been used for revenue control since the early days of railways. At first they recorded passengers' names, as had the mail coaches before them, but when Thomas Edmondson joined the Newcastle & Carlisle Railway in 1839, he devised a ticket system so efficient and convenient that it was used by railways all over the world for the next 150 years.

His plan involved preparing (in advance) tickets for his customers to act as a receipt for their money, authorise them to take a specific journey and, at the same time, to ensure that the money taken was accounted for properly. Thomas's printed cards were cut to 2¼in x 1³⁄₁₆in, and this size persisted until the advent of the microchip.

In the days when Edmondson tickets were used almost exclusively in the UK, many collectors saved only that type, but to do so deprives the enthusiast of hundreds of interesting and unusual ticket issues in different formats. Most people at first collect anything and everything, but as the accumulation grows they tend to specialise. One leading collector restricts himself to the pre-Grouping period (before over 120 companies were amalgamated into the Big Four – GWR, SR, LMS and LNER). Many choose to specialise in a region, county, company or line in which they have a particular interest.

In the 1950s and 1960s Dr Beeching's and other economy drives encouraged enthusiasts to travel the country to ride on 'last trains' and to buy a souvenir ticket. Happily, today, station or line closures are rare and collectors are more likely to seek tickets from newly opened or reopened stations, preferably on the day of opening.

To the uninitiated, British Rail's standardisation of APTIS (All Purpose Ticket Issuing System) in the 1980s may seem to have resulted in a range of visually similar

**Above:** *Thomas Edmondson, inventor of the classic railway ticket.*
***Author's Collection***

**Above:** *Tickets soon produced their own sub-industry. This engraving from the* Illustrated London News *of 1845 shows an early ticket printing machine with samples of its work.* ***Author's Collection***

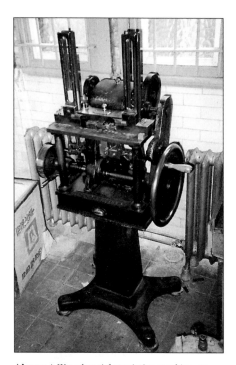

**Above:** *A Waterlow ticket printing machine, now preserved by the Irish Railway Record Society in Dublin.* **Author**

(and perhaps boring) tickets, but it is surprising how many variations can be found. The APTIS family includes the SPORTIS paper variety, usually issued on trains, Quickfare (self-service) and PERTIS (giving Permission to Travel in penalty fare areas). The APTIS credit-card size tickets have appeared in more than 200 different base-print forms for seasons, railcards and special facilities, and the system offers an almost unlimited variety of ticket types, station names and discount codes in the information added upon issue through the validating machine. Alongside APTIS, travel centres, agencies and telesales outlets issue the larger Tribute ticket to ATB size, as standardised by airlines.

Another choice which may be made is whether to collect by station or by ticket type. With the former system you have some

sort of target to reach – a specimen from (or to) every station which has ever existed. Comprehensive lists are available, including subtle changes of title or resitings.

Collecting by ticket type is more of a challenge, as despite the availability of a wide range of official and unofficial publications it is never possible to produce a definitive list. Old documents of the Railway Clearing House, set up to regulate the sharing of revenue from passenger and freight among the many different private companies of old, are helpful in defining which ticket types may be available.

However, there has been no Stanley Gibbons of the railway ticket world, which not only means we have no definitive listing but also few guidelines for values of tickets. Thus it is impossible to suggest how much you can expect to pay for any individual specimen. Prices in dealers' lists and those reached at auctions will give some idea, but the level is often dictated by just how much some individual wants a particular ticket.

When buying tickets in postal auctions (or bidding postally in public auctions) a reserve is usually set as the lowest acceptable price and then the higher bidding begins. If you want a particular specimen you do not lose out by bidding really high, for you will only pay one step above the nearest bidder.

In a recent auction list the reserve for Edmondsons from open stations began at £2, for those from closed issuing points at £5 and pre-Grouping prints at £8 or £10. The price

**Next page:** *The elaborate booking office at Leicester, seen when gas lighting was being phased out in favour of electricity. In an atmosphere now redolent of railwayana interest, note the low benches so that short booking clerks can reach the tops of the ticket racks, also the deeper ticket magazines at the foot of the racks, for the most popular destinations. The ticket racks themselves make interesting items, especially with the destination labels and fare boards intact, but take up a fair bit of wall space.*
**Author's Collection**

**Right:** *The booking office window at Whitchurch North, showing a typical country station ticket rack and, right, the ticket dating press — a once-essential item at every station.* **Author**

ORIGINAL RIBBON PRESS.
(ORIGINAL PATTERN PRESS).

TYPE BOX WITH TYPE SUPPLIED
WITH EACH PRESS.

PRICE COMPLETE
ON
APPLICATION.

The Ribbon Dating Press, although having been used for a great many years, has been very little altered, and may be said to be the best press for ordinary purposes. It is very simple in construction and seldom wants repairing.

**Above:** *Catalogue illustration of a classic ticket dating press and type box. These come up for sale at times and are eminently collectable.* **Author's Collection**

**Right:** *Close-up of the printing heads on a Waterlow machine in the Crewe ticket printing centre shortly before its closure.* **Author**

**Right:** *The 'works' of a late-generation dating press.* **Author**

**Right:** *Half-snip clippers (with magazines to catch the snips for counting) and some clipped tickets. These large clips were used for special purposes, such as converting an adult ticket to one for a child. The resulting clip allowed the clerk to account for the unpaid half fares.* **Author**

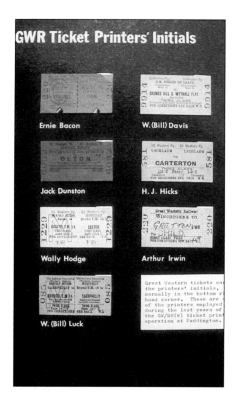

*Above: From an album; the top left ticket features the misprint referred to in the text, bottom right is a training school ticket. Author*

*Above: Album leaf of GWR tickets, with the initials of the compositors included on the ticket face. This gave an added security feature. Author*

achieved will almost always be higher and, for instance, a good example from the Lynton & Barnstaple Railway can go into three figures. Platform tickets have their own values as some people specialise in them, but even so, prices for the last type of BR issue begin at £1, with pre-Nationalisation specimens at £8 upwards.

Most railway and transport events have stalls with second-hand magazines, models and railwayana, where you will often find a small box of tickets at reasonable prices. These events are also likely to attract professional and semi-professional ticket dealers, who are very knowledgeable and almost invariably will help a newcomer to the hobby.

The major source of information and support in the UK comes from the Transport Ticket Society which, with its predecessor, has been established for more than 50 years and supports people who collect all types of transport tickets, not only rail but road, water transport, air and even toll receipts. Membership benefits include a well-produced monthly *Journal* containing news of developments in ticket issuing and historical articles. Members can subscribe to a series of distributions of tickets in the various categories, which are supplied at very reasonable prices – generally the cost of acquisition plus postage. Obsolete ticket issuing equipment is also offered from time to time. A list of members willing to correspond is circulated, showing individual interests, and exchange pools are also operated. Meetings are held in venues around the country, sometimes with a speaker but always with plenty of opportunities to exchange information and tickets.

A fertile source of tickets for a collection of modern types can be tapped by letting friends know of your interest and begging them not to discard any that they receive. Many people keep tickets as a souvenir of holidays or special events and will often part with them to someone who they know will

**Above:** *Four tickets printed for private railways, using a machine now preserved by the Swanage Railway. They feature colour bands which are printed onto the white stock card.* **Author**

**Above:** *Four tickets for unusual forms of traffic: ambulance or hearse (with or without corpse), Lady's ticket, Farm Removal, Tandem.* **Author**

look after them.

As your fame grows you may be invited to buy whole collections – sadly this is usually when the collector has died. More than 15 years ago I read an article in our local paper about a man in our small town who also collected tickets, but somehow never got around to making contact. Recently I received a phone call asking for advice on how to dispose of a collection which, it transpired, was that very man's accumulation dating back to 1938. After arranging independent valuation, I was able to acquire the railway ticket collection, containing much of local interest, and to pass the bus and tram specimens to the TTS for distribution to members.

(Without wishing to become morbid, if you do amass a good collection it is as well to warn your dependants what you want done with them after your death. Some people prefer to have the collection kept intact, perhaps presenting them to a museum or an individual, while others are happy for the tickets to be split up. Whether or not you are a member of the TTS, they are always willing to give independent advice about disposal.)

Today's collectors have a variety of storage and display systems available and it is fairly safe to assume that the plastic will

not react with the printed material inside, unlike the early folders, which spoilt many good tickets when the ink fused to the plastic. A popular type of leaf was originally intended to hold cigarette cards and the version with 10 pockets is ideal for Edmondson cards. Other variants are available, offering between one and 15 pockets per leaf for different size cards. Some philatelists' albums are suitable to hold tickets, and their stock books with rows of pockets are ideal for thin card and paper tickets.

One type of album to avoid is the photo album containing leaves with a peel-back transparent sheet and rows of a tacky latex substance to hold the photographs in place. These react badly with a ticket printed on absorbent pasteboard; the ticket will not be anchored very well because of its thickness and the tacky strips will soak into the ticket, leaving stripes on the backing paper. This form of mounting does not affect photographs, which are not only thinner but generally, today, on non-absorbent plastic material.

Even with modern leaves one should be aware that if tickets produced from machines using a thermal printing process are placed under certain types of plastic, the wording will disappear overnight. My valued

115

**Above:** *Four platform tickets printed by the author for special events. These can achieve good collectable status.* **Author**

specimens of the experimental PORTIS tickets (the forerunner of SPORTIS) from one of my special lines, Bristol Temple Meads to Severn Beach, have faded completely.

The condition of tickets may leave something to be desired and one should always aim to have tickets in mint condition, although this is understandably unlikely with the older specimens. If the problem is surface grime it can often be removed by rolling some white bread into a ball and gently rubbing at the surface. If the paper begins to deteriorate stop immediately, and do remember that Thomas Edmondson's first tickets were printed by inking through a ribbon, which would quickly be erased with rubbing.

Tickets will often be found to have damaged backs from being glued into albums. If a specimen is of particular interest because it is an unusual route or type, this will not affect the value greatly, but never use glue yourself. Most established collectors mount their specimens on white card or thick paper sheets using transparent photo corners. The old gummed type are best, as the modern self-adhesive mounts loosen with age, particularly when holding a ticket printed on much thicker card than a photograph for which the corners were intended.

**Above:** *Special trains often have special tickets. This is an example from a steam-hauled run on BR in 1984. 'Inter-City' tickets of this size were used extensively by the Western, Eastern and Scottish Regions until the advent of APTIS, validated on issue through an NCR51 machine.* **Author**

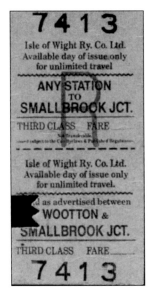

**Above left:** *The final stage of the Edmondson era was the semi-blank, printed with fare and date details in the booking office cash register. This is a South London example. Other region's main stations had machines which fully printed blank Edmondson-size cards at the time of sale.* ***Author***

The condition of the ticket may be affected by quite legitimate clipping and there is much controversy as to whether a ticket is more desirable mint or clipped. I have always been happy to include tickets with clips and for long distance examples the variety of different shaped clips is another interest. When the ticket with which I was travelling was clipped I always tried to retrieve the small piece removed, which could be reinstated in the hole to present the complete printed matter while showing it had indeed been used for travelling.

Sometimes the clipping indicates that the ticket is an audit example, and not legitimately issued for travel. Large numbers, particularly of GWR tickets, are in circulation after being offered by the Western Region to collectors for a nominal sum. Some other railways would part with tickets for collections in return for a donation to a suitable charity — often the Railcare Homes.

When APTIS was introduced, some areas of BR agreed that withdrawn Edmondson tickets could be saved for distribution to collectors after a specific time had elapsed. Thus it is unlikely that audit or unissued examples of the common later varieties will ever become valuable, although they may enable stations or types collectors to add to their accumulation at a reasonable price.

Until BR centralised Edmondson ticket issue at Crewe in the 1960s, all tickets were printed from monotype (traditional lead alloy, with each character on its own piece of metal). In order to fit all the relevant information within the tiny ticket dimensions, it was necessary to use the very smallest size types and so it is not surprising that, despite careful checking, errors did occur. Specimens with mis-spelt station names or other errors can be of interest to some collectors. A favourite example of mine began life as a first class ordinary return between Sheffield and London St Pancras at a fare of £15.98 but was erroneously fed a second time into the machine producing platform tickets for Maryland – and fortunately for me was sold as a platform ticket at 4p! Another error known to have occurred on more than one occasion happened when a ticket left the printers with inappropriate wording on the back. A travel ticket was once issued with the conditions on the reverse relating to the Corporation Baths!

You may decide to expand your collection to include related equipment, from a small item like a pair of clippers to a heavy iron dating press or a ticket rack, which can be a wonderful – if heavy – example of the cabinet maker's expertise.

As ticket systems have been modernised, older equipment has been offered for sale and Collectors' Corner has sold clippers for £5; dating presses can change hands for between £30 and £40. More unusual presses and much sought-after equipment like pull-bar platform ticket machines command high prices at auctions (£1,500 recently), while at the other end of the scale, printing plates formerly used to print Edmondson tickets at Crewe can be bought as cheaply as 25p or 50p each.

When BR closed the Crewe printing shop, the machines, built by Waterlow 50 or more years previously, were offered for tender and were bought by several of the private railways and their supporters. Thus many of the preserved and independent lines continue to use the Edmondson system as part of their re-creation of vintage travel. Other lines have turned to computers to provide revenue figures as well as to monitor passengers; some are little better than a shop

till receipt but the Titan system pioneered on the Ffestiniog Railway produces an attractive paper ticket.

I have so far concentrated on British tickets, but many people collect specimens from all over the world. Edmondson sold his system abroad, first to the French in the 1840s, and the Crown Agents arranged to supply Waterlow printing machines to the colonies. Most foreign countries have, like the UK, mechanised ticket issue, although some eastern European states continue to rely heavily on traditional systems, as do a few of the smaller Swiss private railways and funiculars, which still issue colourful striped cards.

Modern tickets are generally validated at point of sale by feeding a partly pre-printed base card (or paper) through a printer. These can be collected either according to the blank stock or according to the printed matter. A BR APTIS ticket, for instance, can carry two classes, a virtually unlimited number of ticket type descriptions, different 'from' and 'to' stations, routes, validities and railcard or other discount types.

While not as interesting historically as an Edmondson card, many people find them fascinating to collect, and Regional Railways North East even produced pictorial souvenir tickets to make them more attractive. Three designs were issued, all in limited quantities, and if placed side by side will make a single picture.

Standard and normal journey tickets have not increased vastly in value as collectors' items and, as with many forms of collecting, tickets should be enjoyed for their interest and not looked upon as a financial investment for the future; if you do sell at profit, then that is your good fortune.

# CHAPTER 8

# RAILWAY CLOCKS

## by Dr D. R. Parr

*Of all classes of railwayana, a fine railway clock is most likely to be readily accepted into any home, even when other members of the family have little interest in railways. A good clock can be seen as graceful, an item of character in its own right — and useful. David Parr, a specialist in the field, introduces and guides the reader through the complexities of the classic railway clock, and warns the intending collector of some of the pitfalls.*

Among the plethora of collectable railway artefacts, clocks have several appealing features. These make them readily acceptable to many people and also better long-term investments than more specialised railway hardware. They serve a useful function in telling the time with reasonable accuracy, without the need for batteries or a power supply. Many are older than most railwayana, often dating from the 19th century, with a few going right back to the earliest days of railways.

## Types

Almost every type of clock imaginable found use on the railways, from large turret clocks with bells and dials several feet in diameter to small mantel clocks of only a few inches. However, most types were used in tiny numbers and more remarkable than the variety is the preponderance of one type, known as the 'English fusee dial timepiece', which composed a comfortable majority of the clocks used on Britain's railways, and which will be the major subject of this

chapter. The other type of clock which I shall deal with at some length is the 'weight-driven wall regulator' which, while widely used, was found in smaller numbers.

In general, the older the clock, the more interesting. Few 20th century railway clocks, although well made and sound, are inspiring and I shall concentrate on pre-Grouping examples.

## Location

The railways used clocks in many different locations. The most obvious were stations: on platforms, in booking halls and booking offices, stationmasters' and various other offices. In the 1880s the London, Brighton & South Coast Railway had a standard issue to the normal country station of an 18in longcase for the platform, a 14in trunk for the booking hall and a 10in dial for the signalbox. At the other end of the scale, an inventory of Victoria, carried out in 1932, listed 47 clocks. At the Grouping the North Eastern Railway had 34 clocks at York station and over 390 in use at all its locations in this city.

**Fig. 1:** *Two 8in mahogany dial clocks typical of thousands supplied by John Walker to the LNWR, LSWR, GNR and other companies over many years and now much sought after because of their size. Walkers used a variety of addresses over the years, ending up on South Molton Street in 1912 where it still trades today, having moved from No 1 to No 63 in 1983. Walkers probably supplied more clocks to the railways of Britain than any other single firm. While the LSWR adopted the Walker number as its identifier, the LNWR applied its own numbers on vitreous enamel plates but normally left the Walker number on the dial thus leading to potential confusion among those not familiar with railway clocks. The LSWR clock above retains its pre-Grouping dial writing; it dates from about 1873 and was used in Honiton station box. The LNWR clock below was supplied in about 1898 but its location in use is not known.*
**Author's Collection (above)**
**Private Collection (below)**

### Numbers

From records, it can be reasonably estimated that about 50,000 mechanical clocks were in use on Britain's railways by the mid-20th century. Mechanical clocks were brought by the railways from the earliest days right up to the early 1960s and it is remarkable that the basic design remained unaltered throughout this period.

### Survival

While a few clocks have been accidentally destroyed or lost through fire or theft etc, and some by bombing in World War 2, and in later years some were discarded as beyond repair, it is likely that most, including those from the earliest days, have survived – I believe that 60–80% still exist today. A very few are still on the railway system but the vast majority are in private hands.

### The English Fusee Dial Timepiece

In horological circles 'English' is a generic term and includes Welsh, Scottish and Irish; although 'British' is not normally used, it would be more accurate.

Larger stations often had a turret clock in a tower or other prominent place. Signalboxes always had a clock by the edict of the Board of Trade. Towards the end of the 19th century it became normal to have a clock, often a mantel clock, in each office of a headquarters or other important building; the size and grandeur of the clock perhaps reflected the status of the occupant. Railway workshops of all types often had many clocks.

**Fig. 2:** *A very late oak-cased 8in English fusee clock supplied to the Southern Region of British Railways by Stockall & Marples in 1957 for £8 17s 6d plus £2 13s 3d purchase tax. It was used in the booking hall at Aldershot. The dial has been rewritten by Walker's in its role as contractor and also bears the red Arabic numerals of the 24-hour clock which was steadily applied to clocks after this system was adopted by the railways for timetabling.* **P. W. Durham Collection**

**Fig. 3:** *A mahogany 10in dial, one of several hundred supplied to the LBSCR by the Clerkenwell firm of Grimshaw & Baxter between 1873 and 1921. This example was bought for £2 5s 0d in 1901 and used in the parcels office at Clapham Junction before being moved to the Operations Superintendent's Control Room at Deepdene Hotel, the wartime headquarters of the Southern Railway. The dial has been repainted and written in the style found on dials which retain their pre-Grouping writing.* **R. G. Smith Collection**

These clocks have fusee movements, which are relatively large, solid, robust and simple, and with reasonable care and maintenance will carry on working almost indefinitely. The fusee is a grooved, truncated cone, which functions to even out the torque delivered by the spring as it unwinds, and is found only in 'English' clocks.

In strict horological terms a 'clock' has two trains of wheels, going and striking, hence it strikes the hours, while a 'timepiece' has only a going train – it tells the time but does not strike. In early railway days the term 'timepiece' was used for what we now call pocket watches. Almost all railway clocks are strictly speaking timepieces but the railways have always referred to them as clocks, a convention I follow here.

English fusee dial clocks were far from exclusive to railways. Exactly the same design and make of clock was used in many other situations, such as schools and offices, and those from non-railway sources are occasionally referred to by auctioneers today as 'railway' or 'station' clocks, using the term generically.

**Case Styles**

There are two basic styles of case used for English dials.

1. The dial clock (Figs 1–8), also known by railwaymen as the 'roundhead' – an apt description, since they are simple round clocks with the only decoration, if any, being in the moulding of the wooden surround to the dial.

2. The drop dial (Figs 9–19), also known as

the drop case, in which there is a downward projection of the case. The movements are the same as those in the plain dials but the extension to the case allows a longer pendulum, which beats more slowly. In Victorian times this was thought by some to be inherently more accurate. The drop also provides more opportunity for non-functional decoration, which is seen in earlier examples but soon disappeared in favour of a functional design, as the railways became conscious that decoration costs money.

### Drop Dials
The bottom of the drop can curve into the wall (Figs 13 and 18), be square to the wall (eg Figs 9 and 10), or it can be what is accurately described as 'chisel' or 'wedge' (Figs 15 and 17). A very few have flat bases or other more exotic variations. Earlier drop dials often had decorative carved 'ears' either side of the drop, 'supporting' the dial surround (eg Figs 11, 12). As the ears were non-functional and relatively easily knocked off, they have often been lost over the years but the marks where they once were usually remain. Some drop dials have a window in the drop (Figs 12 and 16), through which the motion of the pendulum can be seen. This window is often decorated by applied carving or a wooden or brass beading around the edge. The drop itself also provides an opportunity for the use of attractively figured veneer.

### Sizes
The size of a clock is normally defined by the diameter of the dial itself. The commonest size is 12in, but 10in and 8in dials are reasonably common and are increasingly popular today because of their size. English dials were not made smaller than 8in; 14in and 16in dials occur sparingly, but larger dials than this are uncommon. (All such clocks were made by men working in inches and I refuse to describe a 12in dial as a 30.5cm dial!)

**Fig. 4:** *A late 19th century ebonised mahogany 12in dial typical of many supplied to the MS&L and its associated companies, such as the CLC and the Sheffield & Midland, by the Manchester retailer William McFerran over a number of years. The broad hands and 'easy-to-read' figures on the dial appear to be original to these clocks and not later alterations as they were with the GWR. Ebonising was widely used by the MS&L and the L&YR and was perhaps a sensible finish considering the grimy environment in which these clocks worked in the age when coal was king; it is not to everyone's taste but it does produce an arresting contrast to the polished brass bezel. This clock was used at Marsh Gate Goods signalbox near Doncaster.* **Private Collection**

The use of slightly dished or convex dials, accompanied by a similar convex glass in the bezel, was common in pre-railway days. Their use on railways was rare and examples are always early, probably no later than 1860. The use of brass dials on railway clocks is very rare. Almost all have painted iron dials.

### Case Wood
Almost all English dials are housed in wooden cases. The show-wood is invariably hardwood; the top and back of the box is oak in earlier and good quality clocks, and pine, or occasionally teak or mahogany, in all others. Mahogany and oak are the most

123

common show-woods, while a few were constructed of teak. Anything else is a rarity – walnut and rosewood do occur. Also popular in the Midlands and North was the practice of ebonising – the staining of cases (usually mahogany, sometimes poor quality) to resemble ebony (Fig 4).

The rounded base and drop, if present, are usually veneered, all others parts are solid timber. Teak, and to a lesser extent oak, clocks which were intended for exposed locations, are found constructed entirely of solids, with no veneer (Fig 17).

### Longcase Wall Regulators

One type of clock which, while not unique to railways was largely confined to that use, was the plain, weight-driven, wall-mounted, longcase regulator (Figs 20–25). These were exclusively of British manufacture and contained good quality, single-train regulator movements, with one-second beating, wood-rod pendulums. They were used either on platforms (mostly in the southeast) or within the station buildings but driving a slave dial on the platform. There was normally only one such clock on any station. A few were also used in signalboxes without a slave dial. While some wall regulators were made for use in grand houses, these normally have fine cases and sophisticated movements. Those in railway use, while of good quality, were plain and utilitarian. Such simple wall regulators were used sparingly in other industrial locations but I believe that most were on the railways, especially those which drove slaves. Today the slave has often become separated from its driving clock but you can normally tell by the hole in the backboard, through which the drive once went, and by the modifications to the movement to facilitate the drive.

If any clock can be described as a typical 'railway clock', it must be these plain wall regulators. The normal domestic 'Grandfather' clock, which is floor-standing and has two trains, was not used on the railways.

**Fig. 5:** *A typical 12in dial from the Leeds firm of William Potts & Sons who supplied many clocks to the GNR and the NER although better known now for their turret clocks. This late 19th or early 20th century example shows the normal provincial construction of the dial surround from a ring of eight hardwood segments glued together and based on a displaced under ring of another eight hardwood segments, this in turn glued to an inner ring of pine segments. This contrasts with the normal 'London' surround which was turned from a single piece of timber. This clock was used in the office of the District Goods Superintendent at York.* **Private Collection**

### Longcase Cases

In the southeast, cases were mostly of oak or teak, with 18in or larger dials, and stood about 7ft tall – imposing clocks, one of which is illustrated (Fig 25). In the North, Wales and Scotland they were rather shorter, typically about 5ft tall and constructed of pine, which was originally painted, usually brown, or grained to resemble oak, and nowadays often found stripped; one is illustrated (Fig 21). The dials were smaller, often 12–14in, and frequently 13in in Scotland. Such smaller regulators in mahogany or oak cases are much scarcer, especially those with glazed trunk doors, which were used on the Highland and Great North of Scotland railways (eg Fig 23).

**Foreign Clocks**
While the British railway companies largely bought good quality British-made clocks, there were some exceptions. A number of clocks made in Germany by Winterhalder & Hoffmeier (W&H) in the English fusee style were imported to this country and retailed to the railways. While there are detail differences in cases and movements, which make them readily identifiable, they are generally of comparable quality to the British equivalent, although at the time they were less expensive (eg Fig 6 and 16).

With this exception, foreign clocks were of lighter, less robust design and of poorer quality. Such clocks were available from

**Fig. 7:** *A mahogany 12in dial supplied to the GNR by John Smith of Derby. The dial has been rewritten following the shadow of early writing. The firm became John Smith & Son in 1868, hence this clock pre-dates this. It was used in the stationmaster's office at Ilkeston in Derbyshire.* **Private Collection**

**Fig. 6:** *An early 20th century 12in dial supplied to the L&YR by John Agar of Bury and later Bolton but made by the German firm of Winterhalder & Hoffmeier. The ogee moulded, four-piece dial surround and the hands are among the characteristics of W&H. It bears scorch marks to the lower left side of the surround probably caused by the careless placement of one of the ubiquitous railway oil lamps. The case is of mahogany, probably originally ebonised. It was used in Hoghton signalbox near Blackburn.* **Private Collection**

Germany, France and America, and examples from all three were bought by the railways in relatively small numbers. The Caledonian used a number of American drop dial, going-barrel (non-fusee) pendulum wall clocks from Seth Thomas and the Great Central bought some similar dials from W&H. The Great Eastern used some small wall-mounted brass drum types, also from Seth Thomas, with balance spring (non-pendulum) movements, and the London & North Western used some similar small table clocks in square wooden cases from Württemberg in Germany. Perhaps the most notable user of foreign clocks was, surprisingly, the Great Western, which used several thousand small (often 3½in) brass-cased French balance spring table clocks in signalboxes and offices. These were retailed by Skarratt and later Kay of Worcester, and while often bearing this name on the dial, were also

**Fig. 8:** *An early 20th century mahogany GER dial clock with a 16in dial, a size used frequently by this company, usually on platforms. The dial surround is quite broad, a sure sign of a fairly late clock. This example started life in the Printers Department at Stratford and was moved after Grouping to Colchester MPD. The dial bears the small Ivorine number plate fitted in LNER days to many ex-GER clocks.* **Private Collection**

**Fig. 9:** *An 8in mahogany drop dial with a characteristic square section surround. About 140 similar clocks were supplied to the far west parts of the LSWR system by John Gaydon of Barnstaple and his successor Frederick Fox between 1865 and 1910. This one came in 1890 when it cost £2 17s 6d and was used in Velator box at Braunton on the Ilfracombe branch which was doubled at this date.* **Author's Collection**

marked 'Paris'. They were numbered by the GWR in a separate sequence from their other clocks and the scarcity of earlier numbered examples today is an indication that these clocks had a working life of often no more than 40 or 50 years, it then often being cheaper to replace them than to repair.

These are railway clocks but, with the possible exception of the W&H fusees, they lack the style, quality, interest and reliability of their British-made peers. They were originally bought only because they were cheaper and they should be so today.

## Electric Clocks

While the electrically driven clock was invented in early Victorian times, was commercially available and tried by various railway companies in the 19th century, the clocks used on Britain's railways were

almost exclusively mechanical until well into the 20th century.

## Numbering and Identification

In the early days clocks supplied to the railways were not named or numbered by the owning company.

However, with the passage of time, growth in size, the invention of accountants and less harsh punishments for theft, it became expedient to mark the owning company's name on clocks and identify each by numbering. Such markings were probably first introduced late in the 19th century and the extent and comprehensiveness varied between companies. The pre-Grouping Scottish companies were notable for the widespread absence of company name or number on their clocks.

## Company Name

Many pre-Grouping companies applied their names, usually as initials, to the dials (eg SER, LBSCR, LSWR, GWR, MSL, NER, LYR, GER, NSR, LCDR). In Scotland only the Caledonian named its clocks, by writing on the dial, and then only on some. Some companies stamped or branded their initials into the case (eg GER, NLR, NSR, SER, LYR, GN&GE Joint) and some included the company name on a number plate (eg GWR, NLR, early LBSCR). The South Eastern and Great Eastern stamped their initials on many but not all movements and the North Eastern did on a few. The Midland, despite putting its name avidly on most of its property, rarely marked its clocks in any way and the London & North Western named only some of its dials.

After the Grouping, company names appeared on almost all Southern Railway, Great Western and English London & North Eastern clocks. Some London, Midland & Scottish clocks were named but few if any of their Scottish clocks – or those of the LNER.

## Numbering

Like the Scottish companies, the MR and the GER did not number their clocks – most other pre-Grouping companies did. Only one, the LSWR, which bought most of its clocks over many years from the same supplier, used that supplier's reference number on the dial as its own identifier.

The company number was often written on the dial (eg later LBSCR, GNR, L&YR, NER, M&SL/GCR, LC&DR). The North Staffordshire stamped its number into the case. After Grouping, John Walker, as contractor to most of the Southern and parts of the LMS, stamped clock numbers into the rear of the cases, accompanied on the SR by a letter or letters indicating the pre-Grouping company of origin. Finally, the number could be on a plate attached to the case or dial,

**Fig. 10:** *One of many similar 8in oak-cased drop dials used mostly in signal cabins and supplied to the NER by the long-established Newcastle firm of Reid & Sons over a period of several decades in the 19th and early 20th century. During this period the style changed in minor details but they were always good quality little clocks with several 'London' features including cast-brass bezels and dovetailed joints to the top of the box. This one dates from the turn of the century and was used in Prudhoe station cabin, near Newcastle.* **Private Collection**

some of which (eg NLR, early LBSCR, GWR) also included the company initials.

Number plates were made of several materials:

1. Vitreous enamel, the survival rate of which is generally not good, was used by the NLR, early LBSCR and, most notably, the LNWR.
2. Steel, used by the LMS for early plates and the Lancashire & Yorkshire, which was unusual in also having a separate steel plate on which the location was stamped,

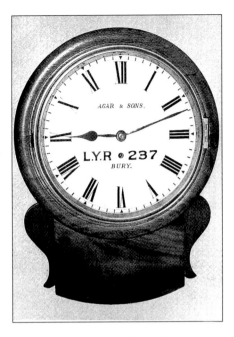

**Fig. 11:** *An appealing little 10in mahogany drop dial with replaced 'ears' supplied to the L&YR by Agar & Sons of Bury. The Agar concerned was Mary who took over her husband's business on his death in 1858, thus dating this clock. The firm was carried on as John Agar for many years subsequently and took to retailing clocks imported from Germany (see Fig 6) but this one is of English manufacture. It was used at Ormskirk just north of Liverpool.* **Private Collection**

**Fig. 12:** *A late 19th century 12in oak drop dial of a pretty style with carved ears and pendulum window decoration, many of which, in both oak and mahogany cases, were supplied by John Smith & Sons to the Midland Railway. This one was used in the District Engineer's office at Bradford. As with most MR clocks this one bears no company markings. After Grouping it was fitted with an LMS oval brass number plate but even this has now been removed.* **B. E. Amos Collection**

both plates often being pinned to the top of the box.

3. Brass, either solid as used by the South Eastern and later the South Eastern & Chatham and usually screwed to the inside of the side or trunk door, or pressed as used by the LMS for its later plates, and continued after Nationalisation by the London Midland Region.

4. Commencing in the early 1920s, Ivorine (a form of plastic), used by the GWR and by the LNER on some ex-GER and most if not

all Scottish ex-North British and ex-Great North of Scotland clocks. The GWR plates were screwed or pinned to the case and the type was continued after Nationalisation by the Western Region. The LNER plates, rather smaller, were often attached to the dials of ex-GER clocks and to the cases of Scottish clocks.

After Grouping, the SR, GWR and LNER numbered their clocks. The LMS in England and Wales retained the LNWR numbers on that company's clocks and added the clocks of the other incorporated companies (principally the MR and L&YR) to the sequence. They did not number their Scottish clocks, inherited from the Caledonian, Highland and Glasgow & South Western.

**Dial Writing**

In the early days the dials of clocks supplied to railway companies were written with the name and town of the supplier (a legal requirement for a short period during the reign of George III) and sometimes with the supplier's reference number but nothing else. Most companies later added to or replaced this writing with their name or initials and sometimes an identification number. Contractors were commonly employed to look after railway clocks and it was standard practice for the contractor to replace the original supplier's details on the dials with his own name and location, whether or not he supplied the clock initially. This form of advertising was seen as a significant perk of the contractor's job. Consequently the name on the dial today is often not that of the original supplier. It should also be noted that the name originally on the dial was often that of a retailer rather than the actual maker who, in many cases, remains anonymous.

Most railway dials have been rewritten, some several times. The rewriting may have been done after repainting, or after rubbing off earlier writing. In the latter case, the shadow of the earlier writing often remains. Dials with pre-Grouping (I always hesitate to claim it to be 'original') dial writing are unusual and those with pre-Nationalisation marking are not common. Either is clearly a desirable feature. The dial is arguably the most important factor in the appearance of a clock. Many have become damaged to various degrees and I believe it is unreasonable to expect any but the ultra-purist to gaze permanently at an unattractive dial. Fortunately there are procedures which allow the scruffy but historically significant dial to be retained but covered by a more presentable copy.

**Fig. 13:** *A 12in drop dial with an attractively figured mahogany veneer on the drop, the base of which is incurved. This late 19th century example is typical of many supplied to the GWR by Kay & Co of Worcester and its predecessor J. M. Skarratt & Co. This one bears the GWR Ivorine number plate on the front of the drop and the dial retains what is probably the original dial writing, now somewhat rubbed. The disappearance of the GWR clock records makes it impossible to say where this clock was used.* **Private Collection**

**Fakes, Marriages, etc**

Because railway clocks carry a price premium, there are always those who will seek to present perfectly good non-railway clocks as of railway origin. Since the basic design and construction of railway and non-railway clocks are the same, the difference arises in the provenance, mainly provided by railway company markings and numbers. It is relatively easy to write 'GWR' on the dial of a non-railway clock and claim that it was

**Fig. 14:** *A 12in drop dial in an oak case with well-figured veneer on the drop. This mid-19th century example has ears carved with oak leaves and acorns and was supplied to the Midland Railway by Thomas Rock of Derby. It has no MR markings and its oval brass LMSR number plate has been removed. It was used in the paint shop at Derby Works, a provenance determined only by the fact that it was sold from there and bears scratched markings on the case with the exact location.*
**Author's Collection**

**Fig. 15:** *A good quality 12in mahogany drop dial with chisel foot to the drop, ogee moulded dial surround and displaying its GWR Ivorine number plate applied in or soon after 1922 when the GWR took over care of its own clocks. It is unusual in retaining its original hands (cf Figs 13 and 18) which are characteristic of the supplier John Walker. Walker held the GWR contract between 1853 and 1871 which dates this clock. It is believed to have been used at Kidlington station.*
**R. A. Gorringe Collection**

used by this company. Equally easy and slightly more convincing is to take one genuine GWR clock with the dial so marked and with a GWR number plate, and transfer the plate to a non-railway clock, thus producing two 'GWR' clocks. Such practices, while not widespread, do occur.

Another problem is that of marriages. Often this involves the insertion of a dial and movement from one clock into the case of

another. While the clock will usually work adequately, its value is reduced and this type of alteration is often difficult to detect without taking the clock apart. I am often told that 'Of course these modifications were carried out by the railways'. This is true, but it did not happen to any great extent and this sort of argument is convenient to explain modern jiggery-pokery. A significant number of railway clocks offered for sale today are,

130

**Fig. 16:** *A late 19th or early 20th century Caledonian Railway 12in mahogany drop dial with an oval pendulum window in the drop, an attractive feature which gives positive confirmation that the clock is going. The dial is written with the company name, the Caledonian being the only Scottish company which marked some of its clocks in this way. It has no other identifying marks or plates and hence it is impossible to say with certainty where it was used. This is another British-style clock made by Winterhalder & Hoffmeier in Germany and has the same characteristics noted in Fig 6.*
**A. J. Lambert Collection**

**Fig. 17:** *An SER 14in oak-cased drop dial with chisel base to the box. It carries its SER brass number plate on the inside of the side door which confirms that it was used in the booking hall at Barham in Kent. It was supplied by Grimshaw & Baxter whose monogram is stamped into the rear plate of the movement alongside that of the SER. It dates from about 1887 which is when the station was opened and was almost certainly bought for that event. The station closed in 1940 and the clock was then relocated to Yeoford in Devon.*
**B. Hart Collection**

to a greater or lesser extent, not what they are made out to be.

**Sources Today**

For many years it has been possible to buy railway clocks direct from BR, notably from Collectors' Corner at Euston, which at times had literally hundreds (although rarely more than a couple of dozen on display). However, all good things come to an end and, with

almost all railway clocks now in private hands, it is from other sources that they must now be obtained. These include private individuals, auctions, professional clock and antique dealers and amateur wheeler-dealers.

As with most other antiques, it is wise to buy from somebody who understands, appreciates and preferably loves the item in which he trades. He should readily volunteer his name, address and permanent telephone number and should be happy for customers to visit his premises. A remarkably high

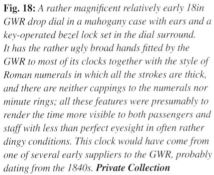

**Fig. 18:** *A rather magnificent relatively early 18in GWR drop dial in a mahogany case with ears and a key-operated bezel lock set in the dial surround. It has the rather ugly broad hands fitted by the GWR to most of its clocks together with the style of Roman numerals in which all the strokes are thick, and there are neither cappings to the numerals nor minute rings; all these features were presumably to render the time more visible to both passengers and staff with less than perfect eyesight in often rather dingy conditions. This clock would have come from one of several early suppliers to the GWR, probably dating from the 1840s.* **Private Collection**

**Fig. 19:** *A large and imposing early LBSCR 18in mahogany drop dial with decorative ears, counterbalance to the minute hand and bearing its early vitreous enamel number plate contained in a cast-brass holder. This clock was one of over 30 supplied to the LBSCR by William Wright in 1851 soon after his appointment as the company's clock contractor; many were of this basic design, although most were of smaller size, usually 14in. This one cost £8 and was used in the booking hall at Hastings. Walkers held the maintenance contracts for large parts of the home counties for many years and like other contractors, applied its name to the dials of all clocks which it maintained irrespective of who supplied the clock in the first place. Hence Walker's name on the dial does not necessarily mean that they supplied the clock originally.* **Author's Collection**

proportion of the respectable end of the clock trade are essentially mechanics, with little or no appreciation of the age and history of the 'machines' in which they deal.

At the less respectable end of both clock and railwayana trades, as with most others,

there are those who are only interested in making as big a profit as quickly and with as little effort as possible, and to whom veracity is an inconvenience readily brushed aside.

A reputable dealer with a love and knowledge of his wares will often (but not

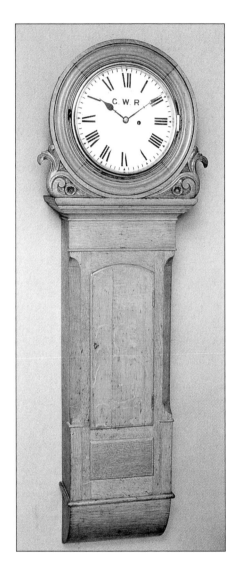

**Fig. 20:** *A 12in oak wall longcase regulator 61in tall of a style used by the Cambrian Railway and possibly other railways in this part of Britain; the details of the carving of the ears varies somewhat between clocks. It hung in the parcels office at Machynlleth in mid-Wales and drove a slave dial on the down platform and probably dates from the opening of the station in 1862. It became GWR property on Grouping in 1923 and consequently now bears a GWR Ivorine number plate screwed to the inside of the backboard.* **Author's Collection**

**Fig. 21:** *A typical pine-cased Scottish weight-driven wall regulator. The case is 57in tall and is now repainted in the shade of dark brown in which many such clocks were originally finished. This mid-19th century example has a 13in dial, was supplied by Fergus Garrick of Stranraer and was used in the signalbox at Stranraer Harbour Junction on the Portpatrick and Wigtownshire Joint line. The inside of the case bears the pencilled details of signalmen who worked the box over many years, a common feature of these clocks.* **Author's Collection**

always) be more expensive than other sources but will still provide 'good value'. He will guarantee both the mechanical and structural soundness and the genuineness of the clock: he should provide an objective assessment of the merits or otherwise and be prepared to buy the clock back at a guaranteed price. He should also have ensured that any restoration work on the clock has been carried out with traditional materials using traditional methods, and adhering to current standards of conservation. I see far too many clocks which have been 'restored' using modern glue, polyurethane varnish and other similar abominations. There is currently only one professional clock dealer and restorer in the UK who specialises solely in railway clocks.

Auctions, both specialist and general, are great fun and a good source of railway clocks. However, while it is certainly possible to get a bargain at auction, or to buy a rather special clock, it is also possible to make mistakes. It is generally forgotten that the auctioneer, despite often charging a buyer's premium, works essentially for the vendor, and, while most are honest in their catalogue descriptions, they are not obliged to point out what is wrong with the clock and often they will not know (or want to know). Some defects are obvious during viewing, others are not. I buy many clocks at auction every year and make some mistakes. I do not sell my mistakes to customers, I put them back into auction. *Caveat emptor!*

## Prices

There is little point in discussing prices in detail since they will quickly become out of date, but, as a guide, a sound 19th century English fusee railway clock, properly restored, guaranteed and with a history, is unlikely to cost less than £1,000 today and in the medium and long term its value is likely to increase. Prices have risen considerably in recent years, a fact probably related to the cessation of the steady stream of clocks which had been coming from the railway system for decades –

134

**Fig. 22:** *A late 19th century mahogany cased 13in wall longcase regulator 63in tall supplied to the West Highland Railway and used at Spean Bridge. The chisel base to the trunk is unusual for a Scottish longcase, most being flat-bottomed. It was almost certainly supplied for the opening of this section of the line in 1894; similar clocks were used on most of the 1894 WHR stations, driving, as did this one, one or two slave dials on the platforms. It came from James Ritchie & Son of Edinburgh, a major supplier to the North British, and in common with most Scottish railway clocks this example bears the supplier's details but no railway markings other than a small Ivorine LNER number plate attached to the inside of the backboard.* **M. E. L. Bentley Collection**

**Fig. 23:** *A mid-19th century 14in Highland Railway wall-mounted regulator in a mahogany case 56in high with glazed door to the flat-bottomed trunk. This example was supplied by James Ferguson of Inverness; others of the same design came from another retailer in that city — P. G. Wilson. These are among the most attractive of railway clocks but do not bear any railway markings. This one was used at Mulben on the line between Elgin and Keith which was opened in 1858 and the clock probably dates from that time. It was closed in 1964 as noted in pencil on the inside top of the clock hood.* **M. E. L. Bentley Collection**

**Fig. 24:** *A mid-19th century 14in oak-cased LNWR wall longcase used at Penmaenmawr on the North Wales coast near Llandudno. It would have been located within the station buildings and originally drove a slave dial on the platform by way of a drive rod passing through the wall. The oblong vitreous enamel LNWR number plate is screwed to the left-hand ear supporting the hood. The dial is written 'Joyce Whitchurch' but like many of its clocks makes no reference to the LNWR. Joyce was associated with the LNWR over many years and may well have been the original supplier although, like Walkers, they applied their name to clocks which they maintained.* **M. R. Henney Collection**

it is simply supply and demand. The LSWR used almost 1,000 8in dials, the LBSCR over 300 10in dials; almost all have survived and both types were readily available a decade ago but I rarely see any for sale today.

Small clocks are always popular, hence, although when bought by the railways the price was normally directly related to the dial size, today the most popular railway (and non-railway) clocks are 8in and consequently these are considerably more expensive than rather larger clocks. The commonest size is 12in and, all other things being equal, this size of clock is likely to be the least expensive. Anything larger will be more costly but the increasing scarcity of larger clocks is to some extent balanced by their relative unpopularity.

Drop dials are generally regarded as more interesting than plain dials and are more expensive.

The price premium carried by railway clocks is due, in part at least, to demand and the provenance which most have. It thus follows that railway markings on dials and elsewhere add to the value. Some companies are always more popular than others and the GWR and LBSCR clocks tend to command rather higher prices than some of the less charismatic companies. Location is important: a clock from a signalbox or the stationmaster's office at a rural station will have more appeal than one from the gent's at a large terminus or 'room 52' of central offices. The older the clock, the more valuable it should be.

Finally, of course, there is condition.

**Fig. 25:** *A good quality English weight-driven wall regulator with 18in dial in a teak case 86in tall. This example was supplied to the LBSCR by Richard Webster in 1867 when it cost £17 10s 0d and was used on the platform at Warnham near Horsham in Sussex. The rear plate of the movement is engraved 'Webster, Cornhill London', a feature often found on Brighton clocks from this supplier but rarely on other railway clocks. The backcock from which the pendulum hangs is mounted on the backboard independent of the movement.* **Author's Collection**

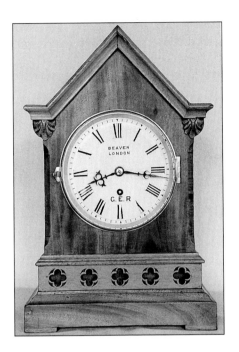

**Fig. 26:** *A late 19th century Gothic-style mahogany mantel clock of a design used fairly widely by the GER. It was supplied by one of the three generations of Beavens to be retained by the GER as clock superintendent. This one, with a 6½in dial and unusually fancy hands, was used in the Advertising Department at 274 Bishopsgate.*
**J. A. Magnall Collection**

Many railway clocks are Victorian; they may have spent more than 100 years in an industrial environment where appearance was of no importance and the only thing that mattered was that the clock did its job. Consequently many have been damaged and repaired; on more than one occasion I have seen scorch marks, presumably caused by the ubiquitous railway oil lamp (eg Fig 6). In later years the care and maintenance was neglected and many are dirty and greasy, or have had paint streaked on the case when the room was repainted. Some have been the subject of abuse since leaving the railway; in the past they could be bought for very little and some have been butchered beyond recognition. As with any antique, those in good, untouched condition are few and this should be reflected in the price.

### Conclusion

A well-restored Victorian railway clock can be an attractive and functional piece of furniture with an interesting history. It will have a character of its own and can become an old and trusted friend, the tick making it almost alive. It should gradually appreciate in value. But beware if you are a collector by nature: I started by buying one railway clock – I now have a collection of well over 100!

CHAPTER 9

# STATION AND OFFICE RAILWAYANA

by John Mander

*The running of a railway has always generated an immense amount of specific hardware, a surprising amount of which has survived as collectable ephemera, or indeed as larger items. From office pen-nibs to platform barrows, from uniforms to furniture, the range is wide. Some types of railwayana here were in common public use, others never came under the gaze of any but railway staff. John Mander, with the experience of years of collecting, introduces a complex subject.*

Many readers will still be able to remember the appearance of major and even medium station platforms dominated by V-shaped wooden signs above the entrances to public and private rooms. If you were still in doubt you could look at the doorplates: in the very early years enamel, then cast-iron and in modern times back to enamel and then fibre. These signs guarded the entrances to the lairs of porters, the telegraph office, foremen, ticket inspectors, inspectors, and the holy of holies, the stationmaster.

**Pens, Nibs and Pencils**

Inside many of these offices, both on and off stations, there lived myriads of items of railwayana. Until quite late in the 19th century, everything appears to have been written in longhand by armies of scribes. To accomplish this, the railways ordered huge numbers of pens, nibs and pencils. We know much about the North Eastern's stock habits, as far more of their nibs survive than for

other companies. They had at least 39 different nib types over the years, as our drawings show (assuming that the numbers on the nibs are not manufacturers' codes). The Great Eastern used at least 30 and it is reasonable to surmise that the other great companies were similarly well equipped. Some lines, like the GWR, SR and LNER, kept their supplies in specially marked nib boxes of one or half a gross. One wonders who authorised the letter writer to use a new nib; did they have to put their hands up as we did at school, and ask for a new pen? Study of some of the nib designs shows that some were very basic, like NER No 3 or GNR No 4, while others were longer and calculated to give a better result, as with GCR No 7 or LNER M9743.

Pencils comprised another part of the railway office world. They came in all hardnesses for a variety of purposes, often with their railway serial number, as with nibs, but sometimes with the maker's name

**Above:** *A display of inkwells, an ink-stand, nib boxes, pencils, etc.* **From the collection of the late Peter Rogers**

**Right:** *Various pencils, showing their company or BR markings. Some give a clue as to use.* **Author's Collection**

**Below:** *A box of nibs from one of the GWR's regular suppliers. Macniven & Cameron were better known to the public as the makers of 'The Pickwick, the Owl and the Waverley' nibs.* **Author's Collection**

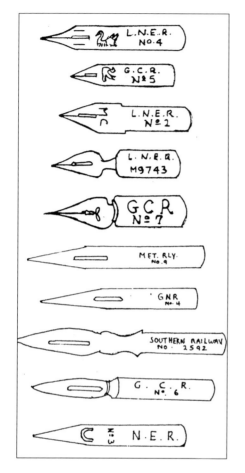
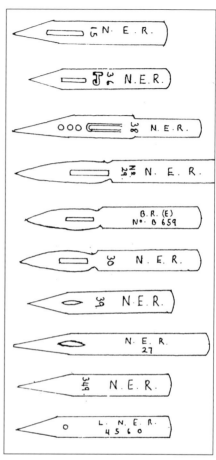

**Above:** *Drawings of some of the various pen-nib types that have come to light in recent years. The variety, in shape and detail, is enormous, especially when bearing in mind that these represent only a small fraction of the total of types that must once have been available! The largest of all is the SR No 2592, whose shaft rather resembles a Maunsell loco tender-side in lettering.* **Author's Collection**

**Right:** *Details of four pen nibs now in the GER Society Collection. It remains uncertain, as manufacturers have closed down, whether the nib numbers were a railway reference or one used by the makers (though often these used letter codes or names).* **Author's Collection**

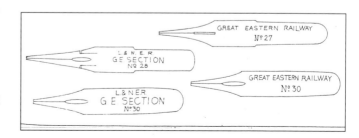

**Above:** *In the days when nearly everyone smoked, provision of ash trays was almost automatic. The style of the simple pressed steel office one contrasts sharply with the crockery example which, from its advertising, was originally supplied to a catering room. (Left:) British Transport Commission; (centre:) brass with SR shipping flag below; (right:) GWR China.* **Author's Collection**

**Below:** *This iron paperweight leaves no one in any doubt about where it should be.* **Author's Collection**

**Bottom:** *Office string tin of L&YR origin. The ball of string inside feeds out through the hole, to stop it being an unravelling nuisance.* **Author's Collection**

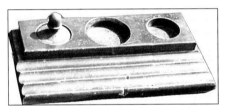

**Above:** *A simple ink stand, grooved for pens and pencils.* **Author's Collection**

**Below***: Offices used pins in large numbers in the days before staplers became commonplace. This is how they were delivered in the early years of the century.* **Author's Collection**

and numbers. Examples are quite common from the NER and GWR but very uncommon or downright rare from most of the other pre-Grouping lines. From post-Grouping times, certain LMS and LNER pencils are almost 10-a-penny but Southern ones are rare. Some of the most interesting are the six-sided GWR ones, presumably made to reduce losses through rolling off desks. Thick blue and red ones were used on outdoor wagon labels and a high percentage of waybills tended to be written in pencil. (This was partly due to the paper or card quality being rather low; ink would be absorbed and give a smudged image. Also, labels might well be filled in outside, where a dip-pen would not have been appropriate.) The LMS issued metal pencil carriers, so that worn-down stubs could be used to the end!

## Rubbers

Company-marked rubbers were issued but survivors are extremely rare. Various patterns are known from the LMS and LNER and recently a whole box of GWR square ones has turned up.

## Office Equipment

A wide range of office equipment was needed, ranging from screw letter-presses to make copies, letter racks, pins, pin trays, bulldog clips for files of letters (the GER was by far the most prolific provider of these), glass and earthenware inkwells, and, more rarely, complete inkwell stands, though few of these are company marked.

## Clothes Hooks

Brass, company-stamped clothes hooks were made for many companies, and going by the large number of survivors, they came in many shapes and sizes too. Some of the better examples had two or three chromed hooks in a cluster.

## Drawer-pulls

Collectors have always been able to acquire marked brass drawer-pulls very easily,

**Above:** *A Manchester, Sheffield & Lincolnshire hinge, clearly stamped with the owning company's initials, in case one went missing and a witch-hunt ensued.* **Author's Collection**

especially NER ones through the Malton auctions. Did the NER really fear that its employees would do some surreptitious unscrewing of their own drawer handles and carry them off home? And the same fear for coat hooks – or was the idea of marking everything an automatic knee-jerk reaction, regardless of the likely risk?

## Carpet or Rugs

The higher status railway rooms were equipped with lengths of carpet or rugs. It was not the practice to have wall-to-wall carpets but rather a rug on top of wooden or solid floors. This practice extended into some waiting rooms and carriages. There are few good quality survivors, for reasons of wear and tear. Pre-Grouping ones are extremely rare and highly valued by collectors.

British Railways continued these traditions to its own design, often adding a totem as its badge of corporate identity.

**Above:** *An LMS rug: such items would be found in first class compartment stock.* **Author's Collection**

**Below:** *Part of a Southern Railway carpet, the company name being neatly woven into the design in the corners.* **Author's Collection**

## Badges, Company Caps and Buttons

It is time to address the railwaymen themselves. This is best achieved by studying the good number of official pictures to see how they dressed or, rather, were dressed by their companies, who had very carefully planned clothes policies for their employees, from the famous bowler hats worn by 'important' people, through Company Police and down via every possible rank. People

*Above right: A British Railways station foreman's badge, Lion over wheel, Foreman in maroon, LM Region. **Author's Collection***

*Right: An example of the famous (and now quite rare) World War 1 Railway Service badge. Railway staff being 'protected trades' in both World Wars, these badges were issued in an attempt to stop the 'White feather' gangs of women from demanding to know why you had not enlisted yet! **Author's Collection***

*Right: Outside porter brass plate armband from the LNWR/MR Joint Birmingham New Street. Outside porters were somewhere near the bottom of the pecking order and the large identity number allowed individuals to be easily identified.*
***Author's Collection***

*Right: Another porter's armband, this one in enamel, from the Midland & Great Northern Joint system and complete with its leather straps. **Author's Collection***

144

**Above:** *Three items from the Lancashire & Yorkshire: medium and small buttons and a van man's cap badge, all in nickel.* ***Author's Collection***

**Above:** *Three painted tin National Union of Railwaymen badges from the later years. Such additions to uniform were not always approved of by the railway companies.* ***Author's Collection***

**Above:** *The standard GWR stationmaster's hat was a fairly grand affair. Should you get promoted to one of the company's really big stations, you could expect something even smarter.* ***Author's Collection***

**Above:** *BR station foremen in earlier days had caps with a wide, stiffened flat top.* ***Author's Collection***

**Above:** *LNER porters, by contrast, had to be content with a more humble soft-top cap.* ***Author's Collection***

**Above:** *Full LMS station uniform set of waistcoat, jacket and trousers, with whistle on chain, correct buttons and a World War 2-style Railway Service badge below a lapel flash.* **Author's Collection**

**Above:** *Provision for dirtier jobs included overalls, as per this LMS Carriage & Wagon denim jacket.* **Author's Collection**

**Top left:** *A large brass button from the Great Northern/Great Eastern Joint line.* **Author's Collection**

**Top right:** *Another large brass button, this time from the Maryport & Carlisle, a small enough company but obviously important enough to have its image pressed into button metal.* **Author's Collection**

**Middle left:** *Carlisle Citadel was the biggest and most important of our pre-Grouping joint stations, so naturally it produced its own signs and uniforms. Even the smallest joint committee would aim to have its own uniform buttons, so naturally the Carlisle Joint Committee was a leader in this field. This is an example of the large nickel type.* **Author's Collection**

**Middle right:** *Another example of a joint station having its own uniform buttons.* **Author's Collection**

**Bottom:** *Flat button, with nicely milled out detail, from the LMS dining car service.* **Author's Collection**

**NORTH EASTERN RAILWAY.**

# ISSUE OF TICKETS.

TICKETS will be issued at this Office, on application, 15 minutes before the advertised time of departure of each train.

GEORGE S. GIBB,

GENERAL MANAGER

**Above:** *A no-nonsense reminder to the public that you cannot expect just to walk in and get a ticket when you feel like it!* **Author's Collection**

**Left:** *Practically every station of any size had a machine like this, or a variant of it, in the booking hall or another suitably public area.* **Author's Collection**

wore badges and did so with pride. These were usually nickel, or brass for higher grades, and were worn across the front of the company cap or, less commonly, on the shoulder or collar, while of course, 'Ambulance', 'First Aid' and 'Look Out' badges were worn round the arms. Some companies issued cloth sew-on badges, notably the GWR. We are still rediscovering ancient examples never seen before. The June 2000 Birmingham Railway Auction had a Midland Railway Senior Inspector metal cap badge, a type never sold before. And people collect, to this day, those famous little coloured tinplate Ian Allan Locospotters badges!

Buttons were issued mainly in three sizes, of about half, three-quarters and one inch diameters, most commonly of nickel, gilt, brass and blackhorn. Generally the largest size is the most sought-after. A fairly high survival rate has occurred, as the number of super-keen button collectors attest to. The various sizes were needed for the waistcoats, jackets, greatcoats, mackintoshes, and all the other garments issued. There are

**Above:** *Midland Railway office chair. This 'captain's chair' design indicates use by someone above common clerk status!* **Author's Collection**

**Above:** *Norfolk & Suffolk Joint Committee chair, probably intended for a public room.* **Author's Collection**

railwayana collectors who specialise in uniform alone and, when you realise the wide variety of caps which existed (and this is only one sub-group) as well as the company-marked overalls, aprons, leggings and even clogs, the scale of the field begins to be apparent. The famous silk top hats of major stationmasters are still a memory (though only just!). Such gentlemen, of course, used highest quality company-marked hat brushes before going on parade.

## Chairs

But life is not all about striding up and down a platform. Much of the time is spent sitting, either as a company servant or as a member of the public. Thus, railway furniture became important at a very early time and wonderful chairs survive from the Bristol & Exeter, the South Devon, the Chester & Holyhead and the London & Birmingham, to name but a few early companies that were later absorbed. Most of the early chairs would have been protected from the weather in waiting rooms, hence so many notable survivors in good condition. Almost always the company initials only were let into the backs; I cannot remember any example of a full name.

The later companies were to carry on this tradition, with the GNR, Midland and GCR well to the fore among known survivors. There are some exquisite examples from joint lines, notably the GN & GC Joint. Lesser examples of furniture were usually marked only on the base with a brand.

There are many mysteries still to be solved as to why we see many survivors from some lines and virtually none from others. The famous Great Eastern swivel chairs are quite common but front-monogrammed LNWR, LMS or LNER types are rare, defying what one might expect in terms of percentage survival of original numbers.

## Long Benches

The major furniture provided on platforms consisted of the long benches we all

**Above:** *Line-up of GWR-family platform benches. The centre one has non-matching castings, a sign of rebuilding in a busy carpenters' shop at some late stage.* **A. A. G. Delicata**

**Above:** *One of the famous and distinctive Furness Railway 'squirrel and grapes' benches.* ***Author's Collection***

149

remember. Alas, few companies provided them with monograms, the main producer by far being the GWR, whose design lasted well into the BR(W) era. There are long and short versions of the intertwined GWR, the roundel and the BR(W) types. Sumptuous designs were produced by the Caledonian, the GER, the London, Tilbury & Southend, the SER and the Furness; most other companies settled for small stampings, findable if you know where to look.

**Sack Trucks and Barrows**
The platforms fairly jostled with sack trucks and barrows which, if unattended, made delightful resting places for us young spotters — until rudely turned off on arrival of authority; we would take off like a flock of crows when shot at, gradually to drift back when calm descended again. Those were the days! Only a limited number of these artefacts were provided with company markings, notably the LNWR/LMS, small strips with 'Euston' or 'Wolverton' on, and the similar NER/LNER plates.

**Poster Boards**
Virtually every station apart from the very smallest halts was festooned with poster boards, used to display the full sheet timetables, company posters by the artists commissioned in great numbers, or day-to-day notices. Apart from the contents, these headings provide a rich source for collectors. The great majority have been made of enamel in a brilliant collection of colours, forming thin strips along the top of the board. They lasted right up to the end, with British Railways producing them in every regional colour, with variants for 'Special Notices' and the rare 'Special Announcements'. These remain avidly collected, with value in proportion to condition, as they are common enough. Some early specimens used cast-iron or lead letters screwed onto wood. I remember a whole block of these in various states of decay at the bottom of a garden in Bath, with the greatest prize being several with Somerset & Dorset letters still on – with at least a good chance that they were originally Somerset Central or Dorset Central Railway (the two being amalgamated into the S&DJ on 7 August 1862).

This, and the illustrations, can only give a taste of a rich field of collecting. Delve into it and you will find many variations on these themes and many more types waiting for you to discover them. Go collecting and keep your eyes open!

**Below:** *Classic example of an LNWR bench, with the station name set into a panel on the back, in raised iron letters.* **Author's Collection**

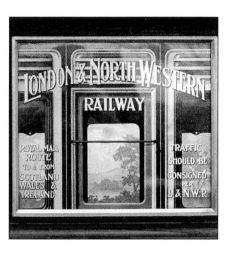

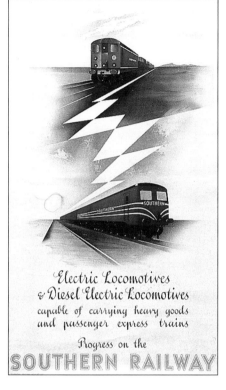

Electric Locomotives
& Diesel Electric Locomotives
capable of carrying heavy goods
and passenger express trains

Progress on the
**SOUTHERN RAILWAY**

LNER    WESTERN HIGHLANDS    LMS
IT'S QUICKER BY RAIL
FULL INFORMATION FROM ANY LNER OR LMS OFFICE OR AGENCY

**This page:** *Four posters, once destined for platform poster boards to advertise services. Shown here in order of age, they give an insight into the evolving styles of publicity departments.* **Sheffield Railwayana Auctions**

The
**DEVON
BELLE**

| | | 12.0 | pm | Waterloo | arr | 5.20 | pm |
| | 3.16 | pm | Sidmouth Jct. | dep | 2.3 | pm |
| | 3.36 | pm | Exeter Ctl | dep | 1.40 | pm |
| | 5.32 | pm | Ilfracombe | dep | 12.0 | noon |
| | 5.36 | pm | Plymouth Friary | dep | 11.30 | am |

ALL-PULLMAN TRAIN TO THE WEST OF ENGLAND
with Observation Car

NEW!

CHAPTER 10

# A RAILWAYANA MUSEUM

by Geoffrey Woodward

*Geoffrey Woodward describes how a small collection has expanded into the Harpenden Railway Museum, which he and his wife Sue own and run.*

My interest in collecting railwayana started with my grandfather's Midland Railway and LMS badges and buttons from the days when he was a signalman. Also, with railway people knowing of my family railway background, access to local signalboxes was easy and I developed an interest in signalling. I managed to collect several signal arms and other parts when they were being replaced during renewal work. In those days old equipment and fittings were simply thrown out.

As a result of a letter to BR in 1963, asking about buying relics, Jack Waldock of Hertford came to see me, with a selection of items from the Hitchin S&T (Signals and Telegraph) depot. That was it; I was away – and so was his collection.

By now the local branch lines were being run down and all sorts of souvenir items, fittings, equipment and other things became available from staff or the scrap men, just for the asking.

Later in the 1960s we put on an exhibition of local railways at our town library and this resulted in more items being given to us. Then of course there were visits to the recently opened Collectors' Corner at Euston and the Roundhouse at Harrow, not

forgetting that MUST for all collectors, the sales at Bitton, Bristol.

We acquired our second signal in 1976, from the closed Hatfield to Luton branch. It was put up in the garden and a photo showing its new home was published in a local paper. This brought visitors to see it. Soon afterwards we had a book on the Hatfield-Luton line published and this was when things really took off.

Items removed from the line and stored in sheds were given to us and we soon found that we had the beginnings of a museum – a collection which deserved to be seen. We were able to put on a reasonable display (or so we thought at the time) of items from local railways. This kept the public coming to see us, so we put more time and effort into collecting; mainly local items but also anything else we liked the look of.

Most of what we bought was for a determined reason as we began to form a 'collection policy'. We had to like it, it was to make up a set, or to show variations, or perhaps to complete another item, such as a signal. A lever frame was purchased, dug out and moved to our garden to work the signal. Later on, a home-made signalbox was built to house it. By now we had several signals

(tall posts as well as shunting signals), notices (enamel and cast-iron), bridge numberplates, rail chairs, a seat, a few totems and some signalbox and station nameboards. A chance acquisition of some local tickets started an interest in these and in luggage labels; but in all this there was nothing of great interest to the lady visitors.

My wife Sue started to collect catering items in silver plate and china, cutlery and saucepans as well as menus. She then moved on to hotel and shipping interests, all this giving a more balanced collection.

Soon we were opening the garden twice a year, and all the time more people – and relics – arrived. There were a few other similar general collections open to the public, such as the well-known one at Winchcombe and also that at Warwick, and we made friends with the owners of these. Being a carpet fitter with an interest in signalling, the contacts I had formed got me the jobs of laying the lino in the signalboxes at Bridgnorth and Exeter West!

**Above:** *The 'outside' items of the collection are housed in the garden. This view shows the extent to which they blend in rather than dominating the scene obtrusively.* **Author**

My favourite item is Jackfield Sidings South Ground Frame, a small signalbox from the former Severn Valley Railway line at Ironbridge, found when on holiday. It was dismantled and transported in a day, during which we found the date 'September 1898' written on an inside timber. It has now been restored, complete with a lever frame, desk, phone, token instrument and a stove, and looks very authentic and full of atmosphere – even more so at night, with the dim lamps shining on the polished brass.

Once the box was re-erected, we had a letter published in a Shropshire newspaper and got several replies from former staff at Jackfield, along with photographs and paperwork, giving us a link with its past.

One thing we discovered when we opened the garden was that it nearly always

**Above:** *A display of signs along a fence. Totems mix with older and later station nameboards; there are several signalbox plates and, below a range of rail chairs, some cast-iron signs mounted on the wall* **Author**

**Right:** *A neat London & South Western-style distant signal from Dorset, still carrying a wooden arm, makes a striking feature among some cast-iron notices.* **Author**

rained on open days, so when a chance came to build a room, we took it. This gave us a display area 'in the dry' and it was opened by Bob Ballard of Collectors' Corner on 14 August 1992. With display units and shelves, we were now able to show different aspects of the railway, such as china, locomotive fittings and numberplates, carriage prints, telephones and notices.

For our silver wedding anniversary, we rebuilt the garden to try to re-create the feel of the days of the station garden, and to set off the signals and notices to better advantage. We had just finished when we were offered another crossing keeper's hut of GNR origin from Welwyn Garden City. This was carefully fitted in and now creates a lot of interest, showing the conditions that railwaymen endured years ago.

The Hemel Hempstead branch from Harpenden finally closed to freight in 1979 and we wrote a book about it. As a result we now have four name signs from that line, which lost its passenger service in 1947, as well as mileposts and notices and signal arms connected with the line.

Besides just collecting, we keep records of what we have and try to find out more about items in the collection: when made, who used them and any stories relating to them. You have a feeling for something if you understand it.

**Previous page. Above:** *Jackfield Sidings South Ground Frame, rescued a few years ago from the abandoned section of the Severn Valley line near Ironbridge, was first built in 1898.* **Author**

**Previous page. Left:** *The interior of the groundframe now houses appropriate equipment, including an 8-lever frame, instruments, a diagram and desk.* **Author**

**Previous page. Right:** *A Great Western/BR(W) centre-pivot signal nestles discreetly beside an apple tree. These signals were, after all, designed for confined spaces! A gradient post could almost be missed behind it.* **Author**

**Above:** *A wide-ranging display of railway catering items forms one of the inside exhibits — particularly appreciated, as there is a tendency to rain on open days!* **Author**

For instance, signals were designed by people with an artistic eye, and while there was much standardisation, many were individuals. They all gave safe passage to the passing trains. Many became known to more than just signalmen by their official names. Then there is the question of who worked them and maintained them until they were scrapped when colour-light signals came in – and now even some of these are history.

The same can be said of much of the railway scene, from the station furniture, the waiting room with its coal fire, down to who used it and where they were going.

Throughout all this there is an admiration for the quality of workmanship that allowed things to survive with little or no maintenance in later days, but they still lived on, often with enough paint left to allow them to be repaired in the original colour, making them nice to see and handle again.

Other items in reasonable condition are left that way, so long as they are able to survive like that.

We went through the stage of trying to collect every variation of items such as bridge numberplates in all the digits from all the companies, but as ours is a general collection this soon became impossible and now only an example of each company's is kept, unless for a special reason. As the available space decreases we have to give preference to local items and now have a named item from all the stations on the Hatfield to Dunstable branch, closed in 1965, including a GNR handlamp from the obscure Chaul End Halt (1915-18); but even now, after 30 years of collecting, something from Dunstable Town eludes us. Why did everything from there disappear?

**Above:** *An LNER lattice post signal from Harpenden East, with a distant arm added below for display purposes, in one of the more crowded corners of the museum. But there is still room enough to appreciate the exhibits.* **Author**

**Top left:** *A fine Great Northern platform oil lamp, on a short iron post for fitting to the tops of walls etc. This one, self-evidently, came from Cole Green.* **Author**

**Next page. Top:** *A further display of BR totems, mostly with local connections but some from much further afield. Below, the wall gives space for signalpost finials and some more cast-iron signs.* **Author**

**Next page. Bottom:** *A display of signalbox and other telephones plus other instruments, below a shelf which shows at a glance the great range of telegraph pole insulators that have been used in the past.* **Author**

158

**Left:** *The seat is Great Northern, the awning ex-Great Western, the wall lamp has Great Eastern origins, while the Lyttleton lamp on its short post is ex-LNER. A cosmopolitan gathering for a minute's rest.* **Author**

**Below:** *Visitors inspect the collection during an open day at the Museum.* **Author**

We also collect photographs and information on local railways, and put on displays for local shows. We now see ourselves as Custodians of a Collection, rather than as collectors.

The collection is jointly owned by us, Geoff and Sue Woodward, and with the assistance of our two sons and friends we run the open days held several times a year. We should add that we receive no financial assistance from outside bodies.

*The Harpenden Railway Museum is open to the public on a number of pre-announced days per year. Anyone wishing to know opening dates is advised to telephone for information: 01582 713524.*

**Above:** *A truly mouth-watering display of carriage roof-boards, signalling block instruments, repeaters and other instruments, with a case of handlamps and other items, forms part of one of the internal display areas.* **Author**